Spirits Speaking from the Heart

Also by the same authors:

"Unfolding the Lotus"
Spirit Reflections on Mediumship

Spirits Speaking from the Heart

Inspiring Communications through Trance Mediumship

Paul and Eileen McGlone

iUniverse, Inc.

New York Lincoln Shanghai

Spirits Speaking from the Heart
Inspiring Communications through Trance Mediumship

iUniverse books may be ordered through booksellers or by contacting:

iUniverse
2021 Pine Lake Road, Suite 100
Lincoln, NE 68512
www.iuniverse.com
1-800-Authors (1-800-288-4677)

The moral rights of the authors have been asserted
A catalogue record for this book is available from the British Library
The authors can be contacted via their website:
www.tranquilspirit.info
First published 2003 Planetree
New and revised edition 2006

ISBN-13: 978-0-595-38725-0 (pbk)
ISBN-13: 978-0-595-83106-7 (ebk)
ISBN-10: 0-595-38725-X (pbk)
ISBN-10: 0-595-83106-0 (ebk)

Printed in the United States of America

To our Spirit Friends

The Phoenix Group

From Hai

What we give, we freely give. We freely give out of love for you all. And by freely giving what we give out of love, we awaken your love and in this awakening we know the love of each other, a mutual love, which expresses our Reality.

Contents

Part Three

Eileen's Note

The following recordings were made whilst Paul was in trance. In the early days I would pose the questions to Hai, when I sat alone with Paul. We used a mini CD player to record the communications, (with an omni directional microphone) which I later typed and stored on our PC. As time went on, we developed around us a committed group of friends who sat, sometimes twice weekly and prepared a variety of questions ready for Hai and the other spirits, who came to talk to us. As our website developed we began to receive requests from other people to attend our circle. We also received questions, (sometimes from people on the other side of the world) submitted via the website. We have therefore over the years collected a large variety of answers to questions put to our spirit group, many of which I would never have thought of asking myself.

Naturally with such a large number of people attending the sessions and or submitting questions on our website some overlap with the questions asked has often occurred. Also different people might ask the same or similar questions to more than one spirit. It has been interesting to note that when this has occurred we have often been given a different slant or way of looking at a particular problem or question. However, the basic answer has remained the same. We have found this particularly helpful when trying to grasp a new concept, which the spirit group have provided. I have known some questions to be asked time and again and each time I feel I understand the answer a little better.

In my previous occupation, during the course of my career, I attended many in-service training courses around the same theme. Repeated material often cropped up but I always seemed to come away with some information, which I didn't have before. It is well recognised that we all learn in different ways, by different methods. We can often be told something several times and not fully grasp its meaning, then someone will explain it to us again in a slightly different way and we will say, "Ah I understand now."

This is how it has been for us with our patient Spirit Group. They have never complained about repeating answers to questions that they know we have asked before. We have always experienced their deep love and respect and they have told us repeatedly that it doesn't matter what we have or haven't done in the past; they still love us.

We know that all of our regular Home Circle members, visitors to our home and people who have submitted questions via our website have all played a part in the publication of this book. Without you all, we would quickly have run out of questions and so both the Phoenix Spirit Group and we are extremely grateful for all your help and support.

It is possible that some of the information in this book has already been covered in other books. If this is the case then I hope the answers here will offer you a new perspective on these issues so that you too can say "Ah yes I understand now."

Many people have written to us and asked Hai to tell them what their purpose in this life is. His answer is always the same: "You can fulfil your purpose in this life every minute of every day, simply by loving one another."

I will wish you well in your search for truth and hope that the information in this book will support you on your journey, as I know our contact with the Phoenix group has supported us on ours.

With love
Eileen

Comments on the First Edition

The following is a small sample of feedback we received following the publication of our first book:

Hi Eileen and Paul,
I am reading the book avidly every spare second I get. Very interesting. Especially how you got started. Hai has such interesting things to say about life, the spirit world, and everything. I have always found his answers to visitor's questions very "down to earth," not esoteric ramblings. Thank you for your hard work, the book, the website and newsletters. They are much appreciated.
Regards
Chris

*   *   *

I've completed reading your book Spirits Speaking from the Heart, and thought I would send a quick comment and thank you. It's very inspiring, not only do we read about how loved we are, we *feel* it. So thank you for sharing your experiences and knowledge to those of us with listening ears.
Marianna

*   *   *

Got the book Paul, enjoying it already, very interesting thanks.
Cameron

*   *   *

Below are two communications received from someone who asked for a postal consultation with Hai:

Dear Paul,
Thank you for your considered reply. I have made a close study of your website over the last two months and am deeply affected by Hai's wisdom. I applaud your work.

Dear Eileen and Paul,

Hai's responses were more than helpful: they were truly inspiring!

AG

＊   ＊   ＊

Reader Review, Amazon:

The grain of sand must stand out…this book does indeed!
A condensed richness of experiences, ideas, philosophy and concepts, that will enable any reader to "get something" at the end of his/her reading. This book is for everybody: from any background…and most importantly, any religion……..

Note on Second Edition

In this revised edition of "Spirits Speaking from the Heart," you will find that the book has received a complete redesign as well as having considerably more information than in the first one. Following the first publication we, quite naturally, continued to receive information from the Phoenix Spirit Group and some of the Guest Speakers featured in that book continued to show an interest in our group. For example, Zeon our Angel visitor paid us two more visits and then Queen Elizabeth the 1st "called in" a couple more times. More recently we had a visit from Charles Dickens and a spirit, Ted, who'd lived on the earth during Queen Victoria's day. Also, prior to our first publication, we'd been given information about how buildings are erected in the spirit world. The information was intended for use in that book; however, each time we received a visit from an architect our mini disc did not, for some reason, record the communication. Shortly after our first edition was published we had two more visits from our architect friends and the disc recorded both.

We had always intended to publish a second book of "Spirits Speaking from the Heart" (book two) when the time was right. However, we were so pleased with the design and (glossy) cover of our latest book, "Unfolding the Lotus" that we decided, instead of bringing out a totally new book later, we would publish this second edition of "Spirits Speaking from the Heart," now.

Acknowledgements

We would like to acknowledge the help and support of all our home circle friends and those, from around the world, who've visited the Wisdom of Hai website. We've also benefited from the opportunity to have taken part in the meditation and development group at Stockport Christian Spiritualist Church and appreciate the encouragement received during the early months of Paul's development.

Most manuscripts require some form of editing before publication and this one was no exception. As is often the case with mediumship, words and sentences can sometimes be repeated for no apparent reason. Hai has explained that this is often done to emphasise a point. However, at other times it happens because the words get caught in a cul-de-sac of Paul's mind, and they go round and round coming out again as a repeat.

We've also found that the language used, especially by Hai and some of the other evolved spirits, can be rather formal. Also the dialect of some of the guest speakers has not always been easy to convey in a meaningful way, in print.

We were keen to ensure that our readers receive the messages from Hai and his spirit friends as they were originally intended and therefore our editing has been kept to the minimum. The editor, Jenny Hewitt has respected our wishes in this. She has spent many hours, over and above what would normally be expected, advising us on numerous matters relating to this work. Between us, we've ensured that only the minimum changes have been made and that the "message" remains intact.

Introduction

By Paul McGlone

The early spring of 1999 saw one of those points in my life where the desire to have concrete evidence of survival came more to the fore. This time I was seeking a more direct and personal experience than that provided by my occasional visits to spiritualist churches over the years.

I approached the venture intending to become an objective investigator of the evidence. Indeed I thought it might become something of a long term interest and hobby, which would continue into my retirement years. In this context one of my first steps was to join the Association for the Study of Anomalous Phenomena (ASAP) as I recognised a need to develop both my understanding of the principles of paranormal research and the skills, which I would require. Little did I think that it would be I that would become the subject of investigation and that the decision to embark on the enterprise would radically transform my life and that of my family.

The enterprise really began to get under way with the purchase of a Ouija board. My wife, Eileen, and I had encountered some early experiences with Ouija boards during our adolescent years—probably the worst time possible to experiment with them. At that time we were both approaching its use in a somewhat superficial way seeking communication with spirits who could answer the personal and worldly concerns that pre-occupy the minds of teenagers. Therein lays the dangers of the device as too many superficial spirits are around waiting to take advantage of an opportunity to play on the fears and desires of human minds by creating mayhem with their mischievous, nonsensical and occasionally malicious responses. I had not myself had any disturbing experiences with the board, though a friend had become extremely disturbed merely by the very idea of the board's purpose. This prompted my mother to return the board to the shop from which it had been purchased. Eileen had become worried when she found that she was able to operate the board on her own, the indicator travelling around its letters at great speed.

Therefore the device has its critics, and to a certain extent with good reason. Anyone who uses it to seek answers to mundane personal questions is foolish and will probably get trouble from the superficial spirits who are only too ready to exert their influence. Likewise I would never advise anyone who has any mental health difficulty or is significantly open to suggestion to make use of the Ouija board. A strong mind is called for and a willingness to dismiss what is being communicated as "rubbish" if that is your conclusion.

In spite of the potential difficulties, we believed that the Ouija board offered the best possibility of communication with other entities. I had not previously had any indication of the slightest psychic ability. Indeed I had recently undertaken a test for psychic ability on the Internet and achieved a depressingly low score. Not that this bothered me, as remember, at this point I was viewing myself as a budding investigator. We were also aware that many seekers starting out on the path to explore spirit communication, including a number of famous ones e.g. Betty Shine, had used the Ouija board.

Actually purchasing the Ouija board proved much more difficult than we had expected. We scoured likely sources in the UK without success. We then turned to the Internet and the United States and found a number of outlets for a surprising variety of boards. The ease of Internet credit card shopping made it possible for the board to be delivered to our Stockport home a mere two weeks later, just in time for our Easter holiday on the Costa Brava.

Forty-eight hours later found us settled into our hotel with our two friends who had come on holiday with us. Our daughter having found her entertainment for the evening, we gathered in our bedroom and opened the Ouija board box for our first experiment. We followed the instructions, imagined ourselves encircled by a brilliant white light and firmly stated our good and serious intent and our desire to make contact with the highest spirits.

We had only limited space so we had to place the board on a small coffee table between the two single beds. The cramped, uncomfortable conditions with the beat of the disco music invading from a couple of floors below made for less than ideal circumstances. However, almost immediately the board's indicator started to move and we found ourselves communicating with a spirit who named himself as the father of one of our friends. What followed was some of the clearest and most detailed communication, which we were ever to obtain with the board.

Our experiments became an almost nightly event for the rest of the holiday with further communication with the father along with communication with some other spirits who took on more the role of guides, their communication having a more philosophical emphasis.

On our return home, Eileen and I started to sit on a regular basis two to three times a week. It was not long before we were contacted by a number of spirits, who indicated that they were working together as a group. At that time the leader of the group called himself Lopaz and indicated that when he had been incarnate he had lived on a planet in a different galaxy to our own. The clarity of the communication through the board was variable and much of the time the spirits showed a preference for using its symbols and images rather than the letters. At times, therefore, communication could be hard work and frustrating and sometimes resulted in misunderstandings over meanings or inaccuracies of detail; at others there could be substantial clarity.

The other spirits in the group who made themselves known in those early days were "Eileen" (who later corrected this to Isleen), who stated that she had previously lived in "Iceland" (which again was also to be later corrected to Ireland). Davia, who stated that he had lived in Papua New Guinea while on the earth plane, Carol, who described herself as having lived in Ancient Roman times and "WB," who has always seemed reluctant to provide us with his full name, and has described himself as a scientist who had previously lived in Scotland. All of them seemed to have their own unique personality and it wasn't long before we regarded them as well known friends. The themes, focused on love, wisdom, and dealing with the difficulties of human life.

Occasionally we sat again with the friends who had been with us on our Spanish holiday. The quality of the communication again could be variable, but sometimes it was extraordinarily clear with the indicator moving rapidly around the board. We were often struck by the continuity of the experience between Eileen and me sitting on our own or with our two friends. The same spirits communicated in the same vein and with the same amiable manner. This consistency, the coherence of the communication and the definite way in which the indicator moved around the board gave us confidence that we were indeed in communication with spirit beings. We were sceptical of the minute unconscious muscle movements and group consciousness theories, which attempt to provide explanations for the Ouija board experience based upon the present level of scientific knowledge.

We got used to a regular pattern of communication with our newfound friends. Lopaz would come through first and would generally communicate the most. Some of the others would then sometimes come through to talk to us. One night we were unexpectedly stunned by a departure from this comfortable routine. Davia came through to announce that he was standing in for Lopaz who had gone away on a journey. For the next three nights Davia acted as the "Master of Ceremonies." As the communication had progressed I had started to get images, which complemented the communication through the board. I had seen Davia as a calm, laid-back person who would not be flustered by anything. This turned out to be only part of the story.

On the fourth night, Lopaz was back from his journey and immediately introduced us to Hai who had "travelled" back with him. It turned out that Lopaz had negotiated Hai's willing involvement with the spirit group in their work with us and indeed it became clear that Hai was to subsequently lead the group. Hai described himself as a Buddhist monk who had lived in Ancient China. We found that the board's indicator began to move less and less in response to questions and we were informed that they wished us to attune directly to them in order that we may receive communication through images. Sure enough, the images came with a clarity that was surprising. Some were symbols to serve as tools of communication. At other times I received vivid images of scenes apparently from Ancient China or Rome.

Our regular attendance at weekly Meditation Sessions run at Stockport Christian Spiritualist Church was a great help during this development. The Guided Journeys provided by the Church's President, Albert Parker and Linda Shaw seemed to speed up and enhance the development of the communication through imagery.

Then the next phase came. One night the board's indicator started to move in a circular, rhythmic motion, slowly coming to a halt.

Simultaneously I felt what I could only describe as an independent energy filling me, which took me slowly, but definitely, back into my chair. Thus began the process of our spirit friends facilitating a deepening trance state, the practice of which now became a regular feature of our sitting. The spirits also indicated that they wished, in the future, to speak through me. At this stage in the proceedings I was unsure about the form that this would take.

The spirit group's desire that we now communicate in new ways and put the board to one side, was confirmed by Elizabeth Hill when we booked a sitting at the Spiritualist Association of Great Britain in London. Amongst other things, she informed us that the spirits that were working with us had said that we could dispense with "our ritual". She confirmed that the spirits were referring to the Ouija Board.

Many, many hours of patient sitting followed and on many occasions had little sign of further development. However, over time, the energy, which had at first focused on my upper trunk and my mind, now started to focus on my throat and I began to get involuntary movements in that area. During this period I felt that the spirits were experimenting with me, trying to achieve "a good fit". When further development did come, it felt like a "bolt from the blue". One night we were starting a routine sitting when I commented to Eileen that my throat was quivering and almost immediately afterwards, Hai, my guide, spoke his first faltering words.

By coincidence or providence, a short time after this event we had the opportunity to attend some trance workshops with medium, Mavis Pittilla. These proved most helpful, both in consolidating the development and in providing me with reassurance in working through the experiences I was having at the time.

The fluency of the communication progressed rapidly as did the number and variety of the spirits communicating. Our Home Circle came into being and while it is, in many respects, still early days, the last few years have seen wide-ranging developments, some of which seemed to come about almost by chance. One night a member of the Home Circle asked if it would be possible for one of our spirits to give us a guided meditation. Isleen's meditations have now become a regular feature, along with our discussions with an ever-widening circle of spirit friends. While the spirit group has indicated that their main purpose is communication and teaching, they have also encouraged us to sit for physical phenomena. This also has been a long and arduous task; however, we have recently experienced a major breakthrough. We will continue with our efforts in this area in an attempt to provide some concrete evidence, which will convince many more people of a continuing life in the spirit world.

I would not want to paint too euphoric a picture, for we have encountered the inevitable trials and tribulations en route, not least of which have been my own periodic doubts about what is actually taking place. My earlier training in the social sciences and as a lecturer has further fuelled these doubts. The confirming evidence supplied by some mediums has been a great support through all this. Opportunities to sit and talk with experienced mediums such as Stewart Alexander and Mavis Pittilla have also been of incalculable value. Nevertheless, in spite of the difficulties, the positives of our experience have far outweighed the negatives.

We have been continually struck by the interest of the spirit group in us and their unconditional loving acceptance of us with all our imperfections. Yet, from the first they have also spurred us on to try harder in developing our love for others and our own potential. Since our communication with spirit began, Eileen and I have had to learn many new skills, not least because our spirit friends have expressed an interest in reaching outwards to others. Amongst other things this has involved me in learning some initial skills in website design and so Hai now has his own website.

When Hai spoke his first words to Eileen, she was unprepared and therefore had to scribble his words on a scrap of paper. He said:

"I am Hai, yes. We want you to go to the world with love. Will you do it? We want you to write a book."

Here is that book and we hope it will be the first of many.

The Phoenix Spirit Group

One night a new member to our group asked Hai:

Why do you call yourselves the Phoenix Group?
The name is not important in many ways but we chose a name because there is an expectation, especially from you side of your life, that you should have some way of identifying us as a group; therefore, we picked the phoenix symbol to represent ourselves; the phoenix whom rises from the ashes.

The phoenix bird was of ancient origin. It symbolises many things in many cultures and civilizations but above all it symbolises hope. From the ashes the phoenix arises to give hope. And so, as we come into your world with our message of hope, we felt it appropriate to commandeer the name of the phoenix, for this is what we wish to bring you my friends, hope; the hope, which is born of love and compassion, the message of love and compassion.

*   *   *

To help the reader with the background and roles of the individual members of the Phoenix Spirit Group, we offer below a brief description of the main communicators in this book. You can read more about our Spirit Group as you read through this book and in the last few chapters, "Conversations with the Phoenix Group," and Hui Hai, The Buddhist Abbot.

Hai (pronounced Hay)
Hai is the leader of the Phoenix group and is clearly an evolved soul. His reason for communicating with us is to pass on wisdom and teaching. In this book Hai answers many questions about the spirit world and life in general.

WB (first name William but prefers WB)
WB is our spirit scientist who works with the energies of the group during our sittings and he advises on all matters of the metaphysical. Some of WB's communications can sound a little formal; however, as you read through the book you will come to know him a little better and appreciate the lighter side of his personality.

Davia (not his real name but tells us he likes the sound Davia, with the emphasis on the last a)
Davia is the Phoenix Group's manager/gatekeeper. He vets and organises all the "guest spirits" and facilitates their communication through Paul. Davia's second role is to lighten the energies and this the reader will find evident as the book unfolds. When a member of our group (earth side) becomes too serious and the energies heavy, he will often put in his two-pennyworth by passing on his light-hearted banter and jokes through whomever spirit happens to be talking to us at the time. This can often be distracting to the poor spirit who is attempting to communicate with us and they often break off to refer to "him" and what he is saying to them; nevertheless, this does without doubt have the effect of lightening the energies. You will find that in some communications reference is made to Davia's "paddle." This has become a joke with our spirit friends and relates to when Davia last lived in Papua New Guinea and used a paddle for his canoe.

Isleen
Isleen, you might say, was one of the founder members of the Phoenix group. She is a lovely gentle soul who takes us through our weekly meditations. You will some of Isleen's communications throughout this book. Paul received a beautiful image of Isleen and we've tried to replicate that on the front cover.

Red Cloud
Red Cloud is Eileen's Healing Spirit Guide. He is not an original member of the Phoenix Group; however, because of this connection with Eileen, he has regularly answered questions and contributed to discussions about healing.

Carol

Carol is an original member of the Phoenix Group; however, she is, for the most part, happy to remain in the background, "doing her bit," as Hai puts it. You will find some of Carol's communications throughout this book and we've included a separate chapter about one of Carol's rare visits in the "Guest Speaker" section.

Hai's Message

"I wish to write many things about the spirit world, to make it clear to you that it is nothing to fear, that it is beautiful, loving and a return to your home—truly. *This* world is rather the unusual; home from home, which is not your home. This is a place of sojourn, not your true home. Your true home is in the spirit world.

We reach out to you, my brothers, and sisters with loving hearts. The same lifeblood pumps through our veins, through our hearts. We share a common heart, a common blood, and a common purpose. We share a common brotherhood in the One Mind. We reach out to you who live as we once lived upon this physical earth. We wish to touch you with the compassion, which we know, which we have learnt because we have lived upon this physical earth. We reach out to you with hearts of sympathy, with eyes of understanding, with ears of hearing, to the pains, to the troubles, to the confusions, which afflict you, which confuse you as they afflicted and confused us in our turn while we were on your earth. Therefore, we call out to you, knowing from where you stand. We offer you our loving hearts and we would wish that you prevail with your conditions, that you grow in your unfoldment, until we meet each other once more in the spiritual realms.

We burn a candle in the window awaiting your homecoming. We burn the candle in our windows for the love of you, awaiting the time when we may all be together again, to meet, to share each other again."

"Hai"

Part One

The Spirit World

Chapter 1

Arriving in the Spirit World

The Nature of the Spirit World

Hai and the other spirits have regularly painted a picture of great beauty and harmony, at least in the part of the spirit world in which they live. However, they become concerned when they know that someone on the earth plane is unhappy because they have not received a message from a loved one. Following on from such a discussion in our Home Circle one evening, Hai had the following to say:

We wish to convey to you the beauty of the spirit land. It's a beauty beyond your understanding. Harmony prevails amongst all the people. The air breathes harmony. There is a peace which is unknown to you on earth, unless fleetingly so. In the spirit world, the peace is deeper and continuous and is not disturbed or distorted by the conditions that you have here. And therefore, it's a wondrous place of peace and beauty, and it's your heritage, the heritage of all people.

There is more openness and comradeship. This may sound idealistic to you, but that is the way it is. Each realm has its own harmony, the realm in which we live, an understanding, more readiness to help, without the pressures or frustrations and hardships, which you have. It's perhaps too easy in some ways, because we don't have these hardships to combat, to overcome. Nevertheless, it is a beautiful thing this harmony that exists amongst us and we don't forget you while we enjoy it. We reach out, as we want to make you aware of it. Aware not only of how we live our existence in the spirit world but also to make you aware that this is both your heritage, but also at the deepest level it is your condition here also. Love underpins all. Love is the foundation. But in the fullness of time the harmony that exists in the spirit world can also exist in this world.

You must know that we wish you to have comfort in the message, which we convey. We wish you to have trust and confidence in what we are trying to describe and impart to you to give you hope for the future.

You must not allow sadness to restrict your minds or sadness to distort your hope. We were touched by Jane's sadness the other night. We know that she isn't alone in feeling such sadness. But we say to you that you must have faith in the future. Because the world, which awaits you, is formed by love, peace and harmony and you will assuredly rejoin those whom you've lost, with whom you have a bond. This is as sure as night follows day. A bond cannot be negated or be thrown aside. The bond that binds you together here continues in the spirit world. It is a natural law, which transcends and crosses all our worlds. Love is a mighty bond. Love is without parallel. Love cannot be overridden. Therefore this bond unites us, holds us together, and cuts across divisions of time and space. Nothing can stand between love: nothing. It's the very essence of our being. If it is not we must discover it before we can make progress and join the harmony again.

There are those who don't love and they should. Whether they know it or not, all are loved by someone. All are loved by the Creative Force, the Creative Being, who recognises the life of all without question, without exception. But, if they don't feel this, it's a pity, because they **are** loved, no matter what they do. No matter how far they drift from the path or from the Universal Love. They are all within this Universal Love, this Universal Harmony.

Therefore, I say again, do not let loss or regret cut you off from this feeling of boundless love, which you all live within. We encourage you to lift yourself up, to attune yourself to this Universal Love, which is all around you. You may also attune to us ourselves, or beings like us and we will respond. We'll bring a link. We'll bring hope. We will bring our love, which is part of the Universal Love, which pervades all existence in all worlds.

*   *   *

One night Hai attempted to describe the beauty of the spirit world. He told us:

I've lived in the spirit world for a long time. The beauty is beyond parallel. It's far more beautiful than the earth, though I enjoyed the beauty and pleasures of the earth when I have lived on it. The colours, are subtle yet vibrant; subtle; yet vibrant. Alive almost. Indeed they are alive. All is alive. All is alive.

Do you live on pure energy in the spirit realms?

Pure energy? What is that? Pure energy is a concept. The spirit planes are formed of energy. Whether you call them pure or not is a matter for you. They are formed of energy of a different vibration to yours. Yet this vibration runs through your world also because there's a Oneness in all things and harmony in all.

Eileen Asked:

In the spirit world, when you touch your hand or touch your body does it feel the same to you as it does to me when I'm on earth?

It feels of substance. Perhaps not quite the same, but it feels of substance. We're more sensitive to energies that are radiated out on people's spirit bodies and from the environment around us. For all radiates energy, love, and harmony. Therefore we're more sensitive to the energies, which make up the world and the boundaries between us don't appear as solid or as definite as they do to you. This applies to our bodies, as well as to other things around us. We don't see rigid finishes to bodies around us. We're all aware of the underlying harmony, the underlying essence behind all things, within all things, and across all things. But, we are aware of our own being. We are aware that it has a form. But it's more subtle than your body as well. We can link with each other more. In fact we often do so. As close as we get in the physical body we cannot touch each other as deeply, as sensitively, as we can in the spirit world. Your Paul has had some experience of this, with Isleen at first, then later with me. We in the spirit world can touch each other's souls and each other's hearts and it's a beautiful thing. Momentarily, we can link to each other. We can feel each other's hearts and minds in a closeness that's hard to understand when you're still in a physical body, but this is one of the joys that you will experience when you return to spirit. It's a marvellous feeling. A closeness that you aspire to on earth and which you can experience to a degree, but not to the degree, or rarely so, that you can experience it in spirit. Do you understand?

Yes, well, as well as I can.

It's like: If yours and Paul's minds' were two bowls of liquid and somehow a means existed for the two liquids to touch each other and make contact. For that moment it would be hard to say where one mind started and the other stopped. There'd be an intimacy, an oneness, for a brief moment perhaps, but an oneness until the liquids returned to their separate bowls again. And there's not the sense of separateness in the spirit world for, on the earth plane, even when you are close together, there's sometimes that sense of separateness, because your thoughts are your thoughts and you're not aware of the thoughts of the other. No sense of psychological touching, if you like and this is restricted by the limitations of the physical world. So only so much is possible. But in spirit these limitations disappear and it is possible to sense, to touch, at a deeper level.

Sun & Light

One member of the group commented on the lack of sun in England. Hai suggested that the only way to get regular sun was to emigrate south. This led on to the following question:

Is it true that you don't have sun in the spirit world, only bright light?

There is bright light but we can have the semblance of a sun but not as your sun.

And on another night Hai told us:

The light in the spirit land is subtle but bright. As bright a light as anything you know from your sun, but it's a much gentler light.

One member commented that he would miss certain times of the day, for example, the sunrise and sun setting. Hai responded:

Yes but *every* time is a nice time in the spirit land. There is variety in our light also. You should not think of a grand uniformity without variation.

Do you have clouds?

Artistic clouds. (Hai laughs) Ascetically pleasing clouds is a good word for expressing it, yes.

Colours

Hai was asked:

Are there lots of colours in the spirit world?

The colours are beautiful in the spirit land. The colours are one of the most outstanding things, which impress you when you cross the border into the spirit land. The colours are subtle yet vibrant, rich hues beautiful beyond your imagination. The light is bright yet soft, illuminating the whole world. There are no shadows in the spirit world. You might think we would tire of this but it is not so. We learn to appreciate such beauty and not take it for granted. The colours are alive. They are bright. They evoke emotions. They give emotions. They are full of emotions. Our life on the spirit plane is more emotional than yours. We are able to share our emotions more with each other, not just through expressing them through our words, our gestures, as you must rely upon. We can convey these emotions directly to each other. There is no need to use language, sound. We can use these things, but we can link directly. We can share our emotions and communicate our thoughts directly.

*   *   *

Arriving in the Spirit World

Hai was asked:

Who meets us in the spirit world? Is it a loved one or a guide?

It is arranged who comes to meet you. It is natural. It is the most appropriate person who comes to meet you, have no fear on that.

Can you expand on that please, Hai?

It may be many different people. It may be someone you have known on your earthly journey, or perhaps a spirit guide or guardian, who has known you on your journey through life on the earth plane and who will come to help your transition to the spirit plane. But whoever it is, as I say, it is the most natural of things; it is a natural process and the person who comes to you will be the best person for this process of transition.

Where people first go when they arrive in the spirit lands?

There are many places that people may go to for help when they reach the spirit world. We have places where they can recuperate and are assisted and aided by those who have compassion for this work. They may receive help to adjust to their return to the spirit world. There are those who can wait upon them, those who are sensitive to their needs, who know what those who need help, who have left this earth and returned to spirit, require. Many chose to do this work. They are experienced and have compassion. You would probably call these places hospitals, though hospital is not quite the right word. They are centres of rest, of recuperation, adjustment, if you like, to the spirit world. There is no fixed time for people to be in these centres. It depends on need. We do not need to rush in the spirit world. Things are active according to time. When the time and the need is right.

On another night Hai was asked:

What happens when we first arrive in the spirit world? Do we look at our past lives?

You meet those who will aid you with your transition. (Smiles) You do not need any "checking in," we are aware of who is checking in and who is checking out. There must be a period of adjustment, which will vary according to need. Some have need for a greater period of adjustment or, in your concept, for a greater length of time and may be helped by going to a place of readjustment, of refreshment, where they will be assisted to a greater degree. This may be because they have spent their last days on the earth plane in pain and therefore, have more to adjust to with the passing to spirit plane.

But with your question about reviewing your past life, this will be a matter of when it is an appropriate time for this to occur and it may happen on a number of occasions. It may happen at different points in time when you are ready to further review your life and learn its lessons.

Who talks to you about your life on the earth plane once you have passed over? Are they especially assigned for this duty?

There are many in the spirit world who are interested in talking to you but there are guides who have a special role for this. They can talk to you about your past life on the earth plane, what you learnt from that life, how you developed from your life on earth plane and so on.

Do these people make themselves known to us or do we have to seek them out?

They make themselves known when the time is right. But you may seek them out earlier if you wish. It is up to you.

One night Hai was asked a question on a similar theme:

When we go from the earth dimension to your dimension is it possible to get lost, or does someone always meet us?

You are always met. Sometimes people *feel* briefly that they are on their own but there is always somebody ready and waiting to come and guide you, to meet you. You should have no worries on that.

Are we always with the people we loved on the earth plane?

Always is a long time. But you will be able to meet up again with those with whom you have the bond of love. The bond of love, I have said before, cuts across all barriers, all barriers of time and space and the barriers between the two worlds. I use "two worlds" here in a simple sense to convey the meaning but you understand what I mean; the bond of love cuts across all barriers. But if you ask; are you with those you love for all time, in the sense, which you use time here, then this, is not the case because there is ever change, ever movement. There comes a time when, for instance, our loved ones must move forward into other realms and we would not wish to hold them back. Sometimes *they* hold themselves back because of the attachment that they have for those whom they love but change occurs even in our world, though the time scales as you would understand them are much greater.

The important thing is the love that we have for each other. This love is a strong bond and carries on infinitely and while we have this bond of love we can never really feel separated from those we love. You should be aware though also that your present life is like the "blink of an eye." You have many others whom you have loved, whom you have a strong bond of love with, who you do not remember, who you have had lives with in the past, and your love for these people was as great as the love you have had for anyone in your present lifetime. So you view your situation from your *present* vantage point, but as I said before, your present vantage point is unable to take in the wider picture.

*   *   *

WB (Spirit Scientist)

We explained earlier in this book that WB is our "spirit scientist." WB initially came through as a somewhat reserved gentleman with a cultured accent. He stated that he wished to be referred to as WB (for now) He has never disclosed his full name to us; however, we understand from another spirit that his name is William. He told us, when pressed, that he had been a scientist when last on earth and lived around the 1800s. He had worked in a university in Edinburgh and had never married. It was suggested later by other spirits that WB had been somewhat reluctant to come through to talk to us, preferring to remain in the background attending to the technicalities of the sitting. Nevertheless, over the following months, WB did become a regular speaker at our Home Circle and has more recently given an excellent talk, through Paul, at a public demonstration.

He later informed us that since arriving in the spirit world he has met "his dear Sylvia" whom he clearly loves dearly. He has told us more of his somewhat austere life and used his experience to demonstrate to us the necessity for a good balance in all things in life.

Over the last few years, our relationship with WB has developed warmth that we could not have imagined earlier on and he, like all the other spirits in our group, has become a true friend.

When you passed over, WB, did someone meet you who you knew?
Yes, it was a dear friend.
Did you have to go to the resting area?
No, my dear, no. It was not necessary. I came round pretty soon to my new environment, even though I was not absolutely convinced on the earth plane of its existence.
As you were partly sceptic while on the earth plane, did you get a shock?
I wouldn't say that I got a shock. It was more a pleasant surprise. I was open to the possibility. My mind was not fixed, not too fixed.
So it didn't stop you from adjusting then?

This is so. This is so. It is when people come with very fixed minds that they may experience that difficulty and I do not say this "fixed" merely from the point of view of disbelief, but it *may* be fixed from the point of view of belief also. It can cause difficulties.

You mean if someone went over with a particular religious belief?

Yes, if they are predisposed to think of it in a certain way.

When you found yourself in the spirit world where you pleasantly surprised?

Yes pleasantly surprised. It was the only way you could be surprised in the spirit world; "pleasantly."

When people go to spirit and evolve and change over time, how will a loved one cope when they pass over? The person they remember will not be the same.

It is a difficulty. It is a difficulty for those in spirit also who may have changed the most. You all have to get used to change though, don't you? Life is a constantly changing process, which you must adjust to; so this is an extension of the problem that you are already familiar with. Time does not carry the same weight in the spirit lands.

I suppose it must be difficult for people whose children have passed on when still young. Would someone feel that the person was not the person they knew?

You should not worry or concern yourself over such things. The important thing is that the bond of love carries through. The bond of love carries through all time and space. The bond is like steel. It cannot be broken. All else will be overcome. All problems will be overcome because steel holds. The steel holds for you not only with those you know in this lifetime but also those you have known in past lifetimes and whom you will know again. The steel bond holds with them also. All other things are as nothing to this bond. You should not speculate and create problems for yourself. You are told it is chicken for dinner and the waiter brings in the silver platter with its silver cover and you get ready for your dinner and he puts it on the table ready and takes off the cover and the chicken flies out fluttering all over the place, full of life. Life is about the unexpected. It is not a muddy flow. It is not stuck in the rut. Life flows. It is creative. It is changing. And it must change to enable the creativity to come about, for the creativity to work its way through and express itself through the changes of life. If there were not change there could be no creativity. So you must go with the change, go with the flow and steer your course with it. Do not worry about the problems of the future. The problems of the future are illusory and are of your own making.

These are some of the things people worry about, though.

They worry about them from their own vantage point here. But from the broader vantage point, the vantage point that can see the two worlds and all these sides, there are no problems. You talk of people changing, yet in truth it is not a matter of change, but a matter of rediscovery, of people who rediscover themselves, their essence, the beauty within, the gold within. And, in each one of you, there is a precious gem of incalculable value, which is your essence, which is you. This precious gem is ever present. Whatever your circumstances, whatever your failings, or your flaws, this precious gem of incalculable value is there, it is you.

Yes, well now I can see why we should not criticise others.

It is all right to be critical in a helpful way, to help them grow, but there should be no malice in it, or irritability. But we are human; we have our failings. If we are irritable it is because usually we want things in a certain way, the way we see things, our way, or done our way. But of course it *is* our way and it does not mean that it is the best way for everyone.

On another occasion, WB was asked:

Do you have a physical form as on earth?

To us it's a stable form of substance, pretty much as you experience on your plane. But to you of course, from your vantage point, it would appear illusory, insubstantial, though all these things are relative.

*   *   *

Our spirit friends have always told us that they have no need to celebrate Christmas themselves. However, many spirits do celebrate our Christmas with us and this brings them closer to the family and friends they have left behind. Some spirits, though, may not always have experienced a particularly happy Christmas when on the earthly plane and for them Christmas can have an extra special significance in the spirit world.

Eileen asked WB if Sylvia was well and if they were looking forward to Christmas. After confirming that Sylvia was quite well, WB had the following to say about what Christmas in the spirit world meant for him:

I enjoy this time of year for, although we do not celebrate in exactly the same way as yourselves, we do partake of your festivities and join in with them. And I do enjoy them because it was a time when it was not of particular pleasure for me when on the earth plane. But now I have the company of a delightful female soul I am able to partake much more in the enjoyment of the time, of the season, yes, to make up for some lost ground, if you like.

Memories of Earth

Hai was asked:
Do people remember physical pain when in the spirit world?
They may remember pain because it is part of their life on earth; therefore, they will remember pain. But the pain will have been removed of course, on their return to the spirit land. But we may feel pain because of memories, which may be still fresh for us, and we may feel pain when we review our earthly life, experiences and emotions. We may also feel pain when we connect with the emotions of pain and discomfort of those who still live on the earth plane. So we are not free from pain, for we may experience pain because of our own experiences in the past and because of our association on the earth plane with you now. You spoke a minute ago of the pain in Palestine between these peoples and we feel this pain greatly; it rends our hearts.

Accommodation, Transport and Travel

Hai and other spirits have often spoken to us about the environment and circumstances in which they live. We soon became aware, however, that it was difficult for them to generalise, as they have made it clear that there is not one spirit world, but rather many spirit worlds or realms. Even within a particular realm it would seem that there are different regions. Nevertheless, we have been given insights into the circumstances, which prevail in these different realms.

One of the topics of interest to our visitors has been about a spirit's place of abode and how they get about. Here are some of the questions put to Hai:

Do ships and boats exist in the spirit world?
Yes, if you wish them to. There are those who wish to live on boats, who have the experience of sailing on boats on the seas of the spirit world.
You said you have boats on the water.
Yes. In the spirit world many choose to use boats, perhaps because they have an affinity with them from their earth days; so they feel comfortable with boats. Others decide to associate themselves with sailing vessels when they take up life in spirit because they find a newfound familiarity, a newfound sense of well-being when they are on a boat, on the sea or on a lake.
Do some people live in caravans?
Some may choose to live such a life and for similar reasons to why the boat people choose boats. Some feel an affinity to the caravan and what it symbolises. So there is choice you see in the spirit land as to our way of life, as to our means of habitation. There is choice. And this is as it should be, should it not?
In some of the books I've read they suggest that some people don't have a house at all. They don't want a particular place to live.
This is true, because in many ways we do not need houses. We do not need walls. We do not need a hall. But we have these things out of convenience, out of custom, because they give us a certain sense of stability, of familiarity, of being at peace with ourselves. But strictly speaking they are not necessary, because we do not have to contend with the elements as you do, for instance, on your earth.
Are there any parts of the spirit world that have cars and trains in the way that we do here or any other forms of transport?
There are some places where such things do exist, because of the need for them in the minds of those who frequent them. So it is a matter of creation, of desire for creating such things. Of course they are superfluous to needs by any criteria you could apply in the spirit world. But, because the people concerned have a love for such things it is possible for them to continue with that love.

How will they know, how will they realise they don't need them, and move on?

You assume they do not know that they do not need them. This is not always the case. They may well know that they do not need them, but nevertheless they wish to carry on with such things because they are used to them, they have affection for them. You have people on this earth who collect old cars. Strictly there is no need for them because they can get more modern, advanced cars. But they collect them out of love for them.

But what puzzles me is if someone wanted a car it sounds if they would have to be in a part of the spirit world where everyone else wanted a car, wouldn't they?

We have places set-aside for such things. Yes, because we could not have such things all over the place.

And people would reside in those places if they wanted?

Or visit them. Like a trip: a day trip.

So they could live in a part of the spirit world where there was no transport and visit somewhere else to be able to use it for the day?

Yes, in the nature of a hobby.

Do you have pyramids in the spirit world?

We have structures, which resemble a form of pyramid.

Are these structures, which we would understand, or are they just pure energy?

They are constructed, but the process is not as you would know it here, because we have our architects, we have our builders, but, as you imply, structure is more an energy form and is built through the application of energy rather than in your traditional ways of the earth but it has substance. This table in front of me is an energy form and, just so, structures of buildings in the spirit realm are energy forms, but they are of a different density, a different structure than you know in your world.

There must be a lot of work before it finally becomes a structure?

No, no, because we do not have the limits that you have to contend with. We have the power of mind and thought to assist us in all our building activity as with all our other activities. So there is not the labour, the physical labour which you require to put up your structures.

On the earth plane, if we want to alter our house, we have to ask for planning permission. Do you have to do something similar?

There is an order to the building as well as the environment. But we can have quick decisions. We do not have to wait for months on end, waiting for your committees to make decisions. Indeed, although there is a decision made in a manner of speaking, the harmony is such that people would know intuitively not to request or wish to create structures in certain situations.

Do you need to take on an ethereal body each time you move from one plane to another?

You might say so. You might say that we adapt to our environment.

But can you adapt even when you have moved on? Can you still come back from the other planes?

Yes, yes.

Is that the case for everyone who moves on, not just for you and other spiritually evolved spirits who perhaps do not need to reincarnate again?

No, it is a matter of development. As we have said before, you progress to other realms, to other levels of being. This does not mean that you may not rebirth. So the issue of moving between realms is not directly related to whether you rebirth or not.

Property

One night a circle member had been looking at the possibility of buying a new house. He commented on the high price of houses and asked Hai, "tongue in cheek," what the price of property was in the spirit world. Hai responded:

Well you know we do not have to barter over our houses. We do not have to bid for our houses. It is rather a matter of an arrangement. All need somewhere to inhabit, all need somewhere to take shelter, though not from *your* elements but rather somewhere where they may feel that they have a sanctuary, a special place that they may call their own. But this is by arrangement not by passing money from hand to hand.

Can you order your spirit home whilst still on the earth plane?

Hai was clearly amused and replied:

You may put in a bid for a spirit home, but whether you have the capital to purchase it will be dependent upon your life while you are on the earth plane.

So for trading purposes, is it the quality of the life we lead on the earth plane that helps us to acquire a nice home?

You may look at it this way. We would not associate the term, trading, with this phenomenon but you may look on it this way if you wish.

Do people tend to live alone, with a partner or in groups?

You may live on your own, you may live with your family, you may live with friends, or you may live in a commune. You may live in all manner of ways, which personally suits you best.

Note: You can read about how buildings are made and erected in the next Chapter.

Children

Another topic, which we've discussed from time to time, relates to the circumstances of children who have died and then gone to the spirit world. We have been particularly interested in the question of whether they continue as children and mature in a gradual way or whether they become mature spirits straight away.

Hai was asked:

When children or young people pass over do they go on ageing?

Well there is no definitive rule about this for it depends upon the individual person and their circumstances. It may be that the person will grow and mature as you say. If they have died as a child they may grow, they may mature through childhood in a sense, within the spirit lands. This is a facility, an enabling experience for them to help them to adjust to their passing, to their development, because perhaps their transition to the spirit plane was violent, was sudden, unexpected, and difficult. So sometimes progressing through a childhood experience and development within the spirit lands is helpful to them. But, there are more mature souls, who would be ready to take up their full position in the spirit land because even having passed as a child, they are a mature spirit and they can adjust rapidly. This may be because they have been many times before, perhaps because they have chosen to have the experience of a young death so they are more ready for the spirit land experience.

People like hard and fast rules but I say there are not hard and fast rules. There are principles, there are guiding principles, but within this there is much scope for variation. It is divine love, which runs the show. It is divine love, which guides everything.

One night Hai was asked:

I read somewhere that if a child passes over to spirit the appearance of the child will remain, because the body is physical and cannot, therefore, grow in spirit even after being in the spirit world many years.

You may take a form, which suits you, which suits your development, suits your maturity of development. This is not a fixed matter. It is possible to choose, depending upon the development of the person and upon their wishes.

So, when the child's parents arrive in the spirit world, would they see the child as a child?

They may see the child as a child if the child manifests as a child. And in the first instance it is likely that they will do so.

And do they grow to what would be the peak of their life?

Yes. But you should not think of children growing up as in an earth life, because here there is not the need for this. It is not like they are growing up in a physical body. So there is greater flexibility. It is more a matter of adjustment and timing than a matter of physical growth because physical growth is not necessary, is not applicable to the spirit world.

Would they take on the body of an adult eventually?

Yes, when they are ready. And when they are ready will vary perhaps from child to child. It is a matter of adjustment, a matter of adjustment.

Do children go to school in the spirit world?

It is not exactly school as you would imagine it, but they have keepers. Friends, who guide them, educate them, who lead them, who help them to grow, who care for them. There is not the rigidity of routine, which you have in your schools. There are opportunities presented to the children to learn and they are guided in this.

On another occasion Hai was asked:

Do children in the spirit world have a chance to read the latest books that are published on the earth plane, watch videos, or new things that come along to us on the earth plane?
Well we can do better than this, Tom. They can access all manner of things, myriad things. There are all kinds of resources available to them which you would not dream of. They have the history of the world, they have the potential of the world; they have the potential of all the worlds, the other realms of spirit, to explore, to be instructed in. There are all manner of things that they may learn of.
I was thinking more of recreational activities.
Yes they have recreational activities, yes.

A visitor to our circle had been watching a programme about ghosts from a bygone age. She was particularly concerned because some appeared to be "lost" children. She asked Hai:
Is it possible that children could be left on the earth plane after they have died, without getting help?
Many spirits would go to the help of such children. They would not leave them to their own devices. They would make themselves known to the children so they could be brought home.

*   *   *

One night a spirit boy, Timothy came through to talk to us. Later, one member of our Home Circle asked Hai the age of Timothy. Hai replied that he was eight. The person commented that Timothy didn't sound like an eight year old and questioned why the boy had not matured because he'd been in spirit many years. Hai was in good humour and laughingly replied:

This is of no importance to him; (laughs again) he wants to come over as young boy; therefore, he comes over as a young boy to you. The fact that he has been in the spirit world for a long time is neither here nor there, for he wishes to manifest as a young boy and has the freedom to do this. Is it not enjoyable to be able to play the young boy again? It is like, you see; you are able to take on the role of an actor but it is you and your own acting. But instead of manifesting a *pretence* of the way you were when you were a young boy, you can manifest as you *really* were as a young boy. I could also do this if I wished to. Ages are not important; you may manifest at any age you wish, most would manifest at a healthy age.

So in the spirit world do you all look young and healthy?

Yes because we are young and healthy.

Do you recognise each other?

Yes, we would recognise each other whether we manifest as ourselves, or something different. We recognise and can identify the signature.

Pets & "Other" Matters

Hai was asked:

Will my cat be waiting for me in spirit?

It will be waiting for you.

I wondered whether it would be my actual cat, or a thought form of it.

There is not too much difference between this thought form and the real thing because we are all thought forms in one sense of the word in so far as we are all manifestations of the One Mind, and in so far as we are all manifestations of the One Mind we may talk as if we are all thought forms of the One Mind. Therefore, the distinction that you paint is not too serious; is not too substantial. This seems deep to you, I know.

Yes, and I thought it was a nice simple question.

But for you Tom you may rest assured the cat will wait for you.

*   *   *

One night we were enjoying a session of Davia's banter. He often likes to shock us and he did it this time by describing how, when last on the earth plane in Papua New Guinea he would roast his special dish of maggots. The conversation moved on to talking about animals and other creatures in the spirit world. Davia was asked:

Do all these insects and fish in the spirit world, get bored after a while, and move on and do other things?

Davia was still in his playful mood and responded:

Do *other* what Tom?

I don't know. Do they develop into higher species?

Well they get a chance to come back here and shove up the scale a bit if they want to, yes, but they have a pretty good time here, you know.

But they can evolve?

They can go through evolution, yes, to move on up the scale.

So could I have been one of those bugs in a past life.

Davia laughed and replied:

You could have been some kind of codfish or some kind of bug or some kind of spider or something, yes.

Someone else commented:

That's seems to be the only explanation that makes sense to me, that we start as creatures and move up the scale.

You're right there Len, though sometimes you know, you get an awareness, you move up the scale and you move into this new body, this new species, this new form of life and you think; "God what on earth did I want to come into this for? My life was much better in a lower form," yes. So it is not all ice cream * when you move up the ladder, no, but it *is* good for you.

*Len thought Davia's reference to ice cream was interesting. Apparently he'd eaten an ice cream before coming to the sitting and had told no one present.

Fashion

Hai was asked:

Do you have access to things like new books and films, etc?

We are aware of the new creations in your world and are interested in them. It is the same as with you though, not everyone will be interested in them. Some will be, some won't be, but that is the way of life. So some of us are interested in all your developments.

Are some of you interested in our clothing fashions, and if so, do they adopt similar fashions?

No, it does not quite apply in the same way but we note with interest your changes, we note with interest the cycle of change too, which turns around and turns around.

I was thinking about children or teenagers in spirit and wondering if they are able to follow the same interests as when on the earth plane.

There is a, sort of, aftertaste of it, of what they would have been like on the earth plane, during the process of adjustment. This process may vary from person to person and some may take some time to adjust. The needs and circumstances of the spirit planes are far from those of the earth plane; therefore, the interests and needs are not the same. We ultimately have no need of clothes so; therefore, fashion is not so much of the essence.

What does your body look like in the spirit world?

It may look as it looks to you now but it may also look different to what it looks now because the body is more capable of change; therefore, we are more aware of the transience of things, changeability of things. All clothing is provisional and equally changeable and while there will be those who adopt things that you may think of as fashion, it does not have the same interest, or weight, as it does on your plane.

If you wanted your body to look the same as it does here you would probably want to cover it up with clothes, wouldn't you?

Hai smiled and replied:

You may cover it up with clothes but the significance of these clothes is less.

Do people remain individuals in what they choose to wear?

Hai smiles again:

Yes there is no uniform.

So we don't have to wear all white, "floaty" things?

No you do not have to wear white, "floaty things." Nor do you have to carry your harp all the time. (Laughs)

Music

Can you tell us about the music in the spirit lands, Hai?

There is music beyond measure. Some of it comes from the earth plane. Nothing is lost if it is created in the earth plane. Music is created also in the spirit plane so there is much music. In many ways music is the essence of life, in that it supports vibrations; it is in harmony with the deeper vibrations of life.

Musicians are not respected in the spirit world simply for what they have done on earth, for humanity. They made their mistakes on earth just like anyone else and still have much to learn. Nevertheless, they have contributed much to people's happiness.

Food and Drink

You may still be able to have your favourite meal or drink in the spirit world; at least for a time anyway. Hai was asked:

Is it possible, in some parts of the spirit world, that when someone first passes over, they think they are actually eating food, if they want it?

This is possible. There are many realms, many planes in the spirit world, and some of them mirror the earth. And, to an extent, they are necessary sometimes to help people adjust because it is a massive adjustment to return to the spirit world. Therefore, sometimes people need conditions or circumstances akin to the physical world to help them on their way, to progress to higher planes.

I remember, when we talked to someone else in spirit, he talked about having a party because it was his birthday.

Yes. This is often the case. We have parties.

I think I made some comment to him that I didn't think there was food or drink in the spirit world.

That is a matter of choice. We can have food if we wish, if that is what we desire. If that is necessary for our sense of well-being. But people progress usually beyond this quite soon, so that food is no longer necessary. But some people like to mirror the conditions, the circumstances, the behaviour of the earth plane, for they feel comfortable with that. Or they want to feel at one, or attune to the circumstances of the earth plane because they still have loved ones there.

Note: Another spirit, Rab, also describes later on in the book how you can still have food and drink if you feel you need it.

Work

A guest to our circle who was particularly interested in the investigative side of mediumship took the opportunity to ask WB, our spirit scientist, the following:

Do you have a laboratory for experiments?
We have no need of laboratories as such. The whole environment is our laboratory in a way. We do not need specialist facilities in the way you do on the earth plane.
Do you miss that?
No. Not really. (Smiles) There was always lots of cleaning up to do!
Is there any cleaning to do at all in the spirit world?
It is swiftly and easily accomplished when there is.
Where do people meet in the spirit world, WB?
We have plenty of scope to meet with each other when we wish. We can meet out in the open. We can meet in a garden. We can meet in one of our homes. We can meet in the Hall of Learning. We have no limitation to the possibilities.
I just wondered where you would meet for work.
There is not the same distinction, which you have. We come together to do something. We may call it work, but it is in the nature of a joy to us. It is something we have taken on; we have committed ourselves to do, because we enjoy it. We wish to help you, for instance. We wish to express our love in some practical way. And so the difference between work and leisure doesn't exist here as it does often on your plane. We do not have to earn our bread.

On another night Hai was asked about work:

What kind of work would a Medium do when reaching the spirit plane, Hai?
This depends on circumstances, upon their need. They may need a total change of work from the mediumship they have been involved with on the earth plane and because of this need for change, perhaps in order to develop, they need release from their vocation in order to develop. But there may be those who wish to continue to develop their gift in the spirit planes, and may choose to work with those whom they worked with on the earth plane but from the other side of life. We

cannot give firm answers here for it depends upon the individual. There are not the rules that apply to groups of people on your plane because of a role they occupy.

So, if a medium is still interested in mediumship and wants to act as a teacher from the spirit world, this would be possible?

This is entirely possible but it is not something they have to do; it is a matter of their choice.

Recreation

One warm summer evening WB was asked about gardening:

Have you been doing some gardening since we last spoke or some other kind of creativity, WB?

Creativity is more in the mind than in the garden. Though, as you are aware, gardening itself is more a creative faculty of the mind here than it is on your present plane. And, although creativity exists on your physical plane as well, the creative faculty has freer rein in the spirit lands in relation to gardening, flowers, and plants. But my faculty is exercised more in the realms of the imagination, ideas. Creativity of ideas is my particular bent.

I was interested in the concept of the flowers singing when Isleen took us on the meditation.

Yes, a beautiful sound; beautiful sound indeed. If you could enlist the help of the spirit land flowers they would do much for your lightness on these nights—beautiful sounds, joyous sounds.

*   *   *

We've already told you a little about Carol earlier in this book and, as we explained, her visits are infrequent. We were already aware, from another spirit visitor, that Carol had a particular interest in her garden in the spirit world. Therefore, on one of her rare visits we took the opportunity to ask her about her garden.

Carol was asked:

Do you have seasons or do you change your gardens at whim, Carol?

We can change them at whim but if we do then we would leave them for a while before changing them again. When you create something whether it be in the earth or whether it be in the world of spirit you grow to love that thing, do you not, and therefore if you create a beautiful flower in spirit, you love that flower and you cherish it, you wish to see it. You may change it in time but you cherish it for a time.

If you create it does it become real to you?

Flowers are energy and though you dissipate it, you only dissipate the energy, which may then be recreated to form another flower or something else. So, you see, no destruction occurs, merely a transformation of the energy.

And the sounds that the flowers make; is that a creation of your own making?

They have their own individual signature but by creating a flower of particular form, by combining elements of design in the flower, you create its own signature; for the different elements have their own tune that blend together to create a unique signature for the flower. A unique musical note if you like, which may combine with other flowers to create a symphony.

Learning and Development

We often talk to the spirit group about the Halls of Learning or (Records) in the spirit lands. One evening, Gregory, who'd spoken to us before, came again and told us about his job as curator of the Halls of Learning. Gregory also talks about how we might learn from bygone times—and past lives.

Someone asked:

What have you been doing since we last spoke, Gregory?

I have helped to keep up the records. Not that it is like writing the records in a book, you understand. But I help with the organization, the accessing of the records.

What sort of records are they?

They are records of the world. People come to see me and I help them to arrange, that they might access what they wish to access.

Like a curator?

I do not make or keep the record myself but I am there to help others to access them.

Is this like what we were talking of before about gaining knowledge?

Yes. Hall of learning, halls of knowledge, which we keep so that those who are interested may have it revealed to them. Not everyone is interested, you understand, but some are. For those who are we've made it available to them.

So we will be able to look back in history if we want to?

Yes and spend many a happy hour so to speak, looking back in your history.

When you look back do you read the equivalent of a book?

You can *feel*, you can *see*, you can *feel*, you can *hear*. It is like being there but you are not there but it's the next best thing to being there.

But when you have this experience I take it that the other people there are not aware of you?

No. No it is not real, you see. It's a facsimile.

Are the records just for our earth?

No, we have records of eternity—records of eternity, for all the conditions of all the planets, of all the times.

Do you have records of the future?

We have the inclination of the future but it is only based upon what prevails now and we cannot say with certainty what the future holds, for it holds all possibilities.

Are there some things that are definite, that will be?

Some things are, inevitably, likely to be.

Do you have to do something to "switch the spirit on" when they want to access the records?

No, you switch yourself on. *You* access the record, which you wish to see and by virtue of the *wish* to see it, you connect with it. But it is a skill and an art that you must learn. Therefore, you need your guidance, your guides, in developing this facility. But many of us can help you with this, to enable you to access the records, to tune into your skill, to tune into the records. They are subtle.

Is it very hard to do?

No they aren't so difficult but subtlety is needed when tuning in to them, which must be learnt and practiced although it is not too difficult once you have the knack. Once you have learnt how to do it, it is like—how you say—once you've learnt how to swim, you remember how to swim. Once you've ridden a bike, you remember how to ride a bike. So you don't forget once you've learned.

Shortly after, Afran, another spirit, whose last incarnation was in Nigeria, visited our group. He offered us further information about the Halls of Learning and on the benefits of accessing particular historical periods. He used (Paul) the medium's situation as an example and explained that we can all start work on ourselves now whilst still on the earth plane. He was eventually asked the inevitable question:

Have you visited the Halls of Learning?
I have, many times. I've seen many sights. I've looked back in history but you know there is so much history to see, so much to learn, so much to view. You cannot view it all but you can choose what you wish to view, what is important to you. Sometimes it's important to do this. It's useful to look at a certain period of history because it *resonates*. It can answer something for you in your soul because of the concerns of the people in that particular era and the trend, the patterns of life during that time in history. It can give a special message to you; can answer some query in your soul, some conflict, some unresolved tension in your soul. So sometimes it's useful to study some specific period of history, because it answers a need in your soul to help you think things through, to help you to resolve something in yourself. This can also apply while you are on the earth plane but it certainly can apply on the spirit plane because we have easy access to history of the world and other worlds also. Therefore, we can tune into periods of history and learn from them to touch our own soul and help us in our development.

How would we know which part of history to study?
You know in yourself. This one (referring to the medium) is attracted to Roman times because he has something in his nature, in his character, which he must resolve. The dilemmas, the tensions, the conflicts of this time, which he is interested in, is helpful to resolve something within his own psyche, you see. It's the same for all of you. You may find you are drawn to a period of history and the period you are drawn to will reflect some tension, some interest within your own psyche, within your own spiritual self, which you must develop in some way. Therefore, it's useful to be sensitive, to feel for what period of history you are interested in: To explore it a little to see what you can discover about yourself, to see what you can discover about what you

should become, how you should grow and develop. You understand me?

Yes, but I thought Paul's interest in the Romans was because of a previous life?

It may well be that a connection also exists with the physical world of Roman times. But this is not to say that also what may happen is because we have lived through these actual times, have lived through the tensions, the conflicts, dynamics of these times, that unresolved issues are, as well as tensions and conflicts, carried forward. They are carried forward into this life, this present life, which we must still resolve. For the tensions within our spirit, within our soul, had their origins in that earlier life, because of the times in which we lived. So it may work also in this way. It's like two sides of the same coin sometimes. For it can be that it's something in our nature that resonates with the issues, the times of former history, past periods of time. Sometimes that which resonates in our soul about that time and place is because we also lived through that time and place and the issues and the tensions and the conflicts are still with us. They still resonate with us in the **now** of our physical self. So it may work both ways and sometimes may come together.

*   *   *

On another occasion WB was asked a question on similar lines:

Are there other places for education besides the Halls of Learning, WB?

We call them Halls of Learning because they are centres of learning where we may access learning records and so on, but much learning is accessible simply from the communion between us all. From the sharing of knowledge and of experiences, the travelling that is possible between the different realms of spirit. There is much to learn in a variety of ways. So we are not dependent on the Halls of Learning alone.

Would the method chosen depend on the individual's intellect?

This is partly so. It is not very different from your own situation, you know. You also learn in a variety of ways, don't you? You don't depend solely on your libraries, for instance and it is not so different for us. The immensity of learning and the potential of course, is very different and we are not hampered by your physical constraints. We may access knowledge in ways that you would only dream of, but the principles of accessing, of taking in this knowledge, are not so very different.

Do you have a greater capacity for memory in spirit?

Our memories are not as hampered as yours and certainly we don't have the problem of diminishing capacity with old age, which unfortunately you suffer from. If this was not the case, then I fear our memories would have long deserted us, thinking about our long stay here!

People talk of the "Akashic Records." Do such records exist?

Yes, there are records we can tap into, which connect us with the time and experiences of the past, yes.

Do you have to have special permission to access those?

You have to see the "custodian," yes.

*   *   *

Hai was also asked about the Akashic Records. He replied:

Well you speak of this Akashic Record like, it is a book you look up but it is subtler than that, more real than that. It is as if every point in the eternal body reflected, encompassed, all things past, all things present and all possible futures and therefore we may tap into this. But we may tap into it from an experiential level, experiential point of view, whereas the words on the pages in your books that you read are something that is out there in front of you. You internalise it by reading it, by thinking about it and you make it your own. But even so it does not approach the intensity, the intimacy of the Akashic Record, as you call it. So it is best not viewed as a record at all.

How would you describe then Hai?

I would describe it as a vibration and as a nerve centre, yet I cannot find words to do it justice. But you will understand from, my attempt to find words, that it is organic rather than something that is static or locked up in a book of some description.

Do we go to a certain place to find this or do we simply go within ourselves?

It can be accessed in many ways but there are also places you can go to access it if you wish. But these places are not essential to the process.

Chapter 2

Two Spirit Architects

How Buildings are Made and Erected

The following two communications are additions to the first edition of this book and we thought it might be useful to explain here the "history" of the recording of the architects.

We started to ask questions about buildings in the spirit world and how they were erected, when we first began to gather information for this book. Generally, when we ask for information on a specific subject, we've found that the Spirit Group will often bring through an "expert" on the subject, often making some joke like; "it is better coming from the horse's mouth," or something of that nature.

This was no exception, and shortly after our request we received a visitor who said he was an architect. We were delighted with the information he gave us and Eileen couldn't wait to get it typed up for the book. She switched on the mini disc, headphones on, all ready to get started—then—nothing; the disc was clear. Eileen thought she'd forgotten to switch on the microphone so, undaunted, we asked Davia (spirit gate keeper) if he could send us another architect.

Two weeks later another one arrived but again, when Eileen attempted to type up the information, she found a clear disc. It is interesting to note that we were recording all other sessions without any difficulty whatsoever.

There was a long gap before the next architect came to talk to us and during the wait Davia continually made jokes about them all hiding from him when they knew he was on the look out for another "sucker." By the time we eventually managed to successfully record information about how buildings are erected in the spirit world the first edition of this book had gone to print. So here it is—finally, in the second edition.

Johansson

We started the conversation by asking a general question:

What sort of things are you involved with in the spirit world?
I am involved with some of the building work, which you have seen in your meditation, tonight. (Isleen had taken us through a meditation earlier)

Full of anticipation and after a quick check to ensure that the CD recorder was, as far as we could see, working ok, someone asked:

Can you talk to us about buildings then?
Well yes, but this is your third attempt I think. (Laughs) I think you are jinxed.

Johansson then went on to give us the information we had waited so long to record.

We are able to project an image, a three D visualisation of a building onto the part of the spirit land where we are intending to place it. Sometimes we may work with others towards this process so that we may share common ideas about our project and it may be that some ideas are varied in their conception and therefore, we can project in a communal effort to bathe this structure in this 3D visualisation and ask for the light to be drawn down to give it more concrete form. It is as if the energy of light is absorbed into 3D visualisation. The energy structure, which we wish to promote, absorbs this energy and becomes denser, more solid you would say, although solid is not quite the word I would use, but it gives it a permanent structure which will endure.

What happens to the house when someone moves on to another plane?
You may want to give it to someone else, if they want it. You may dismantle it. You may simply leave it for prosperity, for someone else

to occupy at some point in the future perhaps. There are no fixed rules about this; there are many possibilities.

How would someone have a house taken down?

You would do the reverse (ask for the light to be withdrawn) leaving its 3D structure. Its 3D structure is like an imaginary skeleton; therefore, this would dissipate with our wish.

And the same thing would apply to a public building then?

Yes. It shows you that the creative process is ever adaptable, is ongoing. The energy that has been required to fill one building may be withdrawn and used to fill another building. But this does not quite convey the truth of the matter, for in truth it is the same energy, which fills all buildings; they partake of the one essence of energy.

Note: Johansson did expand on this a little further but unfortunately even this recording, in parts, was not sufficiently clear.

Someone commented:

People are very interested to know how buildings are made in the spirit worlds.

Yes, it is a beautiful process to watch and we have many crowds that gather round us, even those who have seen it many times will gather round, for it is a unique experience each time. They do not grow tired of the spectacle; they do not loose the novelty of it for it is unique each time to an extent. It is each time a new spectacle.

Do you have units of measurement in the spirit world?

Measurements are not a problem or obstacle for us. We could create interpenetrating buildings if we wished. There is no obstacle to either.

I take it that your buildings do not wear out so do you change them from time to time just for a change?

We can change them from time to time if we wish, yes. We all like variety don't we? We all like some change from time to time, some new expression of our creativity, of our ideas. Therefore, we can do this if we wish. But we are not given to change for the sake of change.

There would only be so many buildings that would need building wouldn't there?

When you have eternity of space to work with, you have eternity of space to work with, (laughs) yes.

Oh, I see.

So there is no limit. (Laughs again) We are thinking of placing one where you sit.

Do you help to build people's houses as well?

Yes we can help to build people's houses; (with amusement) a simple task compared to the great cathedrals we build sometimes.

Do the colours of the buildings vary as well?

They are beautiful; they are beautiful pastel shades, beautiful gentle shades, but vibrant living energies, colours, beautiful. They speak to the heart of peace.

Do you have staircases in your buildings?

Yes you can use a staircase if you want to or you can "flow up it," (laughs) or flow down it.

You wouldn't actually need a staircase though would you?

No we do not *need* one but we sometimes use one, it's like home.

Can spirits go through spirit walls in the spirit world in the way they can here on the earth plane?

Well they will not generally go through buildings but sometimes we will imagine ourselves in a far place and commute (laughs) by thought to that place. So we do not need to travel through walls particularly, but we could if we wish. We come through your walls all the time.

Well I must be on my way. I am most grateful to you for listening and showing interest in my work.

There followed some brief light-hearted banter about the number of times we had attempted to record an architect from the spirit land. Johansson laughed heartily and replied:

Well you are running out of chances. We cannot keep repeating all this ad infinitum, even though we have eternity to do it. We do not want to be sat here two thousand years from hence, you in your body still, because you were too attached to getting a recording from an architect in the spirit lands. Goodbye.

*   *   *

The Drawer of Plans

A few weeks later another spirit came to talk to us about buildings in the spirit world. We did not get his name and we referred to him later, simply, as the Architect. While he was with us another member of our Home Circle went spontaneously into trance. We did not get his name either but he seemed to enjoy taking part in the conversation. The Architect began the communication by telling us:

> I am a drawer of plans.

This caused some laughter within the group. Given that we'd just had a long wait for the previous architects to pay us a visit it seemed funny to have two speakers on the subject in such a short time. Eileen commented that the mini disc usually played up when an architect came through. This Architect had a keen sense of humour and replied:

> Yes it holds its hand to its ears when it hears of the approach of the architects.

Our guest told us he had been an architect when on the earth plane. He is still engaged in the work but told us that it is a different enterprise now. He continued:

> My skills have carried over and have been useful but it is a different enterprise and I had to adapt them and learn anew, but we are never the worse for that for we must all learn things anew.

Eileen asked if he also could tell us how the buildings in the spirit world were made. He joked first about how our buildings on the earth plane were constructed and then went on to say:

> Our buildings are a different "kettle of fish," different case in point all together. With our buildings we may construct a plan within our minds. We can imagine a form of this building to perfection within our minds. Then we can approach it with this perfect rendition of our thinking, our plan onto space. This may be the space on a table but we may also do this in situ, where the building is planned to be formed, or to be erected, if you wish. And therefore, we can render a full three

D replica of this building but in its framework, in its basic form and later with its full texture, within the place where it will function.

Therefore, we may render this three D "hologram," if you wish to call it that, because it is like a kind of hologram. We would render this hologram that we may see it, that we may witness our creation of our thoughts and we may then modify this creation of our thought before it is rendered solid, so to speak, before it is finally formed. We can make adjustments at this stage to its shape, to its size, to particular aspects of it, certain features, you understand, rather than the whole frame itself. So, we may work on the particular, yet we may also work on the global aspect of the building. And therefore we may continue to make further adjustments until we have this form to our liking as a final form.

We may do this on our own if it is a small building but we may do it as a group of architects with others if it is of a grand and substantial nature and therefore requires the thought, energy and the creation of many minds. We would hold this form, which we have achieved to our perfection, at least our estimate of perfection, then we would call down the solidifying light, solidifying energy, but I speak of solidifying in only a relative sense, you understand. But we would call down this energy that it may take final form and take on a further reality within our realm. Therefore, we would construct these buildings according to their need and purpose just like your architects upon your plane. We would construct a church for its purpose, a library for its purpose, a house for its purpose and so on; we can adjust our mental forms to suit the need of requirements before the energy is called down to make them of an enduring substance.

If someone needed a house in the spirit world what would they have to do to get one?

You know you could build your own if you wished to try this; like your DIY. If you wish for help you have only to send a thought for help and your helpful friends will arrive at your side to do your bidding. The sending out of the thought for help will be received by some and will be responded to by some and they will arrive at your side to do your will.

It was at this point that another medium in our group spontaneously went into trance. The spirit who came through joined in with the conversation. He added for our benefit:

It is like; if you have a passion for something, you are happy to share it with others, and these people have a passion for their architecture as some have a passion for their garden; they love to assist. So they would love to come and help you design and construct your building. It is their passion. It is not that they are in servitude; they just love and wish to give out their knowledge and help you.

The Architect continued:
Yes it is as my friend says. It is like; you are a flower sending out a scent and the bees gather to the honey pot.
Is it true though, that you can only have the kind of house that you deserve according to the life you have lived on earth?
Well yes there are restrictions assuredly upon what is appropriate for your needs and what is deserving but we may all apply (laughing) for a bigger mortgage.
Do some people arrive in the spirit world and find that they don't deserve a house at all?

He smiles and responds:
We would not see them homeless.

Again our second spirit visitor chipped in:
Deserve is a very strong word that is not an appropriate word to use.

The Architect continued:
There are schools of architecture in the spirit world just as you have your schools on the earth plane. One of our number (meaning architects) has spoken before of this, of our mansion. He has gathered about him friends of like mind who live together for the purpose of the study of architecture in our realm, of the appropriate forms. It is a matter of structural harmony but yet it is also a matter of harmony within the environment, you understand. So it is a study not just of the nature of the building, of the composing of the building; I pick the

parallel with music because architecture in our realm is like composing music. But it is not just the composing of the particular building, which is our concern but that this building should be in *harmony* with its environment. So, to a greater degree than on your plane I believe, our study and purpose is to achieve far greater harmony with the overall environment, so that there is a harmony between the buildings we construct and our environment; a gentle harmony. There is no abrasiveness between them.

I understand that when we evolve in the spirit world we go to another part of the same plane or to a different one, so how do you move your home?

Well there is no need for it to move of course. It may be left as a home for someone else or it may be dissolved and another home would be made ready for you on your new plane. There is no shortage or difficulty in this.

Our second spirit visitor added:

Your new home does not have to be the same as your old home; you may adapt it if you wish.

The architect responded:

Yes (smiling) you may be humbler if you wish.

I understand that you do not really need a home in the spirit world.

No, you do not. You may carry your home *within* you. You do not need shelter over your head. You do not need a base. You do not need an anchor point, but many of us are grateful for the opportunity to have these things out of custom, because of our earthly experiences, because our natures thrive with this idea of having a base, a point of return.

At what point would you let go of a home? Would that be when you get to a certain level in the spirit world?

It is entirely up to you what you would wish to do but as you have said, there is no need for it.

It was time for our visitor to depart and he said:

Well I think I have accomplished my mission and I think I must walk back along the path with my walking stick.

Is the stick just for show?

It is to show you what my condition was in the last phase of my life on this plane. I needed a walking stick. Well, I must be on my way to build my next building. Perhaps you will come and admire some of my creations when you come over. I shall arrange a tour of the most remarkable and memorable and I do not make any charge whatsoever.

Note: This last remark was a joke about Davia, our spirit gatekeeper, who tells us he will arrange all manner of tours for us in the spirit world—and the only currency required is a good joke.

*   *   *

Shortly after our visits from the two architects a member of our Home Circle asked Hai if they had computers in the spirit world. As so often happens, the questions continued and expanded into other areas of interest. We've included the communication here because we felt it nicely complemented what the architects had told us.

Hai was asked:
Do you have computers in the spirit world?

Hai's answer was short:
No.
Do you have mechanical devices then?
There is not the same need for mechanical devices like you have on your earth plane, for it is of a different vibration. There are energy systems that connect with each other which are used for various purposes but they are not quite as your machines are, no, they are more subtle, more like energy systems which may interconnect.
So do you use energies to make things happen by blending them together?
Yes, but they *naturally* blend together, there is a *harmony* between these energy systems, so from one point of view it is a bit like your computer programmes, where you can get your computer programmes to work together. It is similar to that but not of the same substance, not of the same density or vibration as a computer system. Yet there are some similarities. When the architects build their houses and are in the different stages of their work they can create, what you would call, a three D model, a representation of the building which they contemplate

and they can make it so it is visualised, perhaps like your hologram, yes, in the space in which it will be, although they can rearrange, manipulate it and place it in different places. They can manoeuvre and adjust it until they are satisfied with it, then they call on another energy system which intermeshes with and cooperates with this representation to create the final building in its more substantial form.

You said once that if someone had a very small house but had lots of people come to visit then you could expand the space to that which you needed. Is that right?

Yes, but space and time do not have the same significance, are not of the same order or quality as in your time, your space. Therefore, it is like; (smiling) the building has elastic sides. We can squeeze more people in should we need to.

If I were watching from the outside would it expand or stay the same?

Well you would not see any appreciable difference. You could have your picnic on the outer walls and it would not be disrupted by the expansion within.

Is that because pure spirit is not physical so you could get as many in as you wanted?

Well, you must know that it is relative what you speak of here for you speak of pure spirit. We are merely on a different vibration, a more ephemeral vibration, you may think from your standing point. But to us there is a more substantial reality to our surroundings.

So it's spirit but not solid?

It is solid, but not physical, of a substance but not of your substance.

So from a spirit point of view are you solid?

It appears of substance. Our world appears of substance to us and the representation of our bodies that we choose seems of substance to us. For in our world we are relative to our world and our world seems of substance.

So could you feel yourself hugging a loved one?

We say that we are of substance so we may both feel each other if we wish or we can connect with each other if we wish. There is flexibility here depending on the way in which we represent ourselves.

So it can be physical or mental, then?

Physical but not physical in your way. Mental but not mental in your way.

So, to return to my earlier question about expanding houses, if you can have these automatically expanding houses that you can fit lots of people in, why would someone want a mansion?

Many architects (laughing) If you wish to have big mansion because you wish to house many architects for instance, a school of architects perhaps, then you might as well build a mansion. It is more fitting for a big school of architects, is it not? But the other condition of which you refer to is useful; it has a function should we need a bigger space for some reason.

Chapter 3

Realms and Levels

We find that the possible number of realms/levels that exist in the spirit world often intrigues people. One member of our Home Circle asked Hai for clarification.

I was reading something about different levels in the spirit world. The book said there were seven levels. Is that a correct analysis or just a simplified version for people?

You should not get too hung up on levels. What you speak of is an approximation, but it's also a simplification. But there are different realms, which you may progress through, and this is what the seven levels referred to. So there is some truth in what you say but you shouldn't take it too literally.

So within each realm there must be many levels, which you can move through?

There is opportunity for progression, for movement to other realms when the time is right, when your vibration has been raised to the level that is in attunement to the other realms. And so we progress. At each realm, its occupants feel a substance to their experience. But for those of lower realms, though this is not a good word to use, the higher realms appear somewhat ephemeral, rather insubstantial. But this is not so for those who live there. It is a matter of vibrations and being attuned, being matched to those vibrations. So your vibrations here of course, as you know, are dense, heavy for us. But these things are relative.

*　　　　　　*　　　　　　*

And on another night a similar question was put to ai but phrased differently. The person asked Hai if there were other dimensions that we didn't know about. Hai replied:

There are many dimensions. It is best not to think of how many dimensions for there are many dimensions all interpenetrating each other, all interlinking each other. Therefore, they are associated with each other, they are not apart from each other, and they are not separate to each other but are *at one* with the whole fabric and are all interlinked.

So will we understand more when we are in spirit?

You will understand more, but it is not purely a matter of spirit because it is rather, a matter of energy systems. And though we speak of the spirit world and of spirit, it is more accurate in the final analysis to speak of energy systems and beings of energy. You are beings of energy. Your world is a system of energy, of a certain type of energy, dense type of energy, yes. But *we* are a system of energy also and our world is a system of energy too. Therefore, there is a similarity but because our system of energy, the energy vibration signature, is different to yours you cannot link with it directly, easily, in your everyday world, everyday mind. Nevertheless, we are all systems of energy and therefore, we share this in common with each other. There are many energy systems. I say this because I not wish you to think in terms of contrast; of the physical world and spiritual world, because they are of a Suchness, fundamentally, in the final analysis.

*   *   *

One night Hai was asked:

As we are already spirits encased in this body are we already on the first level of spirit now?

Hai smiled and replied:

This level of what?

In terms of being a spirit and developing. I understand we develop and go to other levels but as we are already spirit now is earth classed as the first level?

We are all spirits. We are all spirits, as you say, Katherine; therefore, we are all spirits and we are always spirits: first and foremost we are always spirits. So whether we inhabit a body on the earth plane or whether we inhabit one of the many spiritual planes, which exist, we are always spirits first and foremost: there is no discrepancy here, there is no distinction to be made here. But as you say, it is true that as we progress and evolve through the spiritual realms we progress in our own spiritual development, in our own spiritual manifestation. Therefore, our spiritual bodies evolve, become more refined, more attuned to the refined realms of spirit. But we are all spirit fundamentally, when all is said and done, and in the fundamental analysis, we will be no nearer to the One Mind in the tenth heaven than we are in the first. So you are on a plane here, a plane of evolvement. You should also know, that because you are all on this plane of evolvement, there are some of you who are already on a higher level, as you would put it, but this is due to the state of development of their souls, rather than being bound by the distinction of the physical and the spiritual planes. Therefore, all life is spiritual in the final analysis: the ground of all life is spiritual.

*   *   *

Spirits Appearance in the Higher Realms

Below, Hai talks about choice in the spirit world. The question started with a general one about clothes and went on from there to a discussion about a spirits appearance in the higher realms.

Do we get to choose our clothes in the spirit world?

Well you are spirit now, Tom and you get to choose your clothes, so what difference should there be in this matter in the spirit plane. There are many planes of spirit but within these many planes you have choice to choose how you manifest yourself.

Even in the higher planes would you have choice?

Yes. You have choice how you manifest yourself but this, in the higher planes, would not be choice to do with clothes or their semblance. It would be more to do with something else; how you represent yourself, how you manifest yourself.

What do you mean by that? Do you mean what form you take?

What form you take, yes, what manifestation you make of yourself.

So do people in those planes choose to show themselves simply as light?

They can be a form of light, yes. But the manifestation of this form of light can take many shapes; different characteristics, though within this even there is much choice according to need, appropriateness and the benefit that will come from it.

What sort of shapes do you mean? Do you mean humanoid shapes or squares and circles, stars?

All manner of shapes.

But would you retain your individual mind, Hai?

Hai smiles and replies simply:

Individual mind.

Note: Considering the times Hai has talked to us about the One Mind it was hardly surprising that he smiled when he replied with such a short sentence.

The questions continued:

So, a spirit wouldn't manifest as, for example, a light coloured chair or something like that?

A light coloured chair would not serve any purpose (smiling) except for someone to sit on.

I was just trying to get an example that I could understand.

Then a being of light may manifest as an Angel with wings or a being of light may manifest as a holy saint, such as a holy nun or holy monk, you understand?

Hai's Home

One night Hai was asked the following question about the realm where he normally resides. As he described his realm, his voice changed perceptibly and we could almost feel the emotion (and perhaps the longing) for his home. We've also included the questions that followed because we feel that the way in which the answers were given again demonstrates the versatility and good-humoured approach we've come to expect from our spirit friends.

I understand that the spirit world is beautiful but what does your particular realm look like Hai? For instance, has it got landscape or is it just light?

It is beautiful, yes it has. (Referring to the question about landscapes) I can travel between realms. One realm is more subtle, more spiritual, more refined, more—it is difficult to explain in your words. It is more of an affinity with the Essence but in truth this is only a matter of relativity. At other times we have said that your realm is of the Essence too, yet it is easier to *feel* the Essence in some realms rather than others because they are, in a sense, closer to It. Yet, as I speak of this "closer to It" there is danger in misleading you for there is only the One Mind, everywhere present. Yet it is as if—I can only explain it this way to you; if you think of your own bodies, yes, and you think of your own heartbeats, hearts, you can feel the pulse of your blood in every part of your body. You can feel your pulse even at your fingertips, and your fingertips are furthest away from the heartbeat, the heart. But as you travel nearer to the heart, up into the main arteries emanating from the heart, they are much closer and feel the heartbeat more profoundly.

And it is this way I would try to explain to you to make a comparison. So there are realms within the spirit world that are closer to the heartbeat; like as if they were close to the main arteries, to the heart within your bodies. And there are those realms, which are more akin to the fingertips. They all *feel* and *are* of the heartbeat, you understand? Yet some can feel it more profoundly, more closely.

Is there a realm, which is the heartbeat?

The heartbeat is within every realm, my friend.

Is the realm that we will go to, more beautiful than earth?

When Hai replied he seemed like his "normal" self again. He laughed and replied:

Davia's realm is very beautiful, *very* beautiful.

Hai appeared to be listening to someone. He laughed loudly and continued:

He (referring to Davia) does not allow smelly seaweed on his beaches and he does not allow sex on the steps. (see note below)

Note: The last remark about sex was a joke that had arisen from one of our meditations with Isleen and we feel adequately demonstrates that we do not lose our humour when we go to the spirit world. During the meditation, Isleen had taken us to a large building and told us there was an old man sitting on the steps. She asked us to go over to him and offer him something. In the feedback two female members of the group reported that they had simply embraced the man and *felt at one* with him. Davia later told us, that what we had done was the closest thing we could get to our sexual act on the earth plane. The phrase, "sex on the steps," became a standing joke with our Spirit Group and even now Davia will regularly refer (tongue in cheek) to the way we "lowered the tone" of the spirit world with our actions.

*   *   *

Johan

Johan was a spirit Guest Speaker. The initial question put to him was about communication between the spirit and earth planes. However, as so often happens the questions broadened out to cover other things.

He was asked:

How long after moving into the spirit world can you return to the earth plane, to communicate with a loved one?

There are many factors here to consider but as a general principle, you may return for quite some time.

Do you reach a stage when you cannot return?

You reach a stage when it becomes more difficult to return, because you must lower your vibration as we must lower our vibration to come here. Therefore, it becomes more difficult sometimes and the effort may not always be conducive to us.

Do you still have the same possessions, or do you have more or less?

There is not so much need of vibrational forms when you progress into the more advanced refined conditions, but when you are in other realms you feel the need for these things. Therefore, this is another indication, that the other realms are right for you at this point in time, this point in your development. But time will move on. You will develop and when you move into other realms you will not have the same needs as those, previously.

As spirits evolve further and do not have the same need for material things, what do they do? Do they become teachers for others?

They may become teachers. They may become partners in enterprises, in working with the various worlds.

Eileen said it was time to finish. Johan gave us his blessing:

*   *   *

Well my friends, you tell me I must wend myself back home to my possessions, (smiles) so I will be going. I leave you with a beautiful picture of a beautiful sunset. When I was on this earth I looked out often on a beautiful sunset. A beautiful sunset encapsulates the gift of the present day, of the day we have had, a beautiful remembrance of the day we've been given. But as the sun dips below the horizon and the colours become magnificent, we know the sun will return in the morning with the gift of a new day. So I leave you with this, my friends, and I wish you a goodnight and a good day tomorrow.

*   *   *

The Darker Realms
The Message: No one has to stay in the darker realms for ever.

Many of our visitors have asked about the darker realms of the spirit lands. The questions have been varied and have concentrated on many different aspects. Hai has always said that no one needs to remain in the darker realms but it is up to the spirit concerned to follow the "light." He told us; they must first see that their situation is not desirable and begin to wish for something better, as this enables other spirits to help them. The spirit concerned will then have to make amends for the wrongs they have done. However, their living conditions will change as soon as their minds become more positive and they start to make changes.

Hai was asked:
At what point does someone enter the darker realms?
If they are drawn to the darker realms, as you say, then they will be attracted there immediately. They don't go to the centres first. Many

people work in such areas to help these souls, to help the spirits, in the hope that they will hear. Eventually, eventually, hopefully, all will hear, but it takes time. They are often deafened, if you like, deafened to the call from outside, to the love and compassion that tries to reach them. They are not fine tuned to the vibration. They don't hear it. They don't sense it. They are attuned to their own, lower, unfortunate vibration, which is at one with their mental state, the state of their heart. You could also say this is relevant to your condition on earth. You also assume thoughts, create thoughts, patterns, vibrations within you that can block your experience and eventually create darker vibrations around you that block out the light, the joy, which weigh you down. It is not easy to dismiss such thoughts, such vibrations, because, on your earth, conditions sometimes bind you in that direction. It seems at times that patterns of thinking are imposed upon you. Yet we must try to not be subject to such causes as this. We must try to strike out with our own independence and free will, our own thinking, to create more positive vibrations. This is not the condition with which we first started.

Those that are in the dark realms have the result of a life of creating dark thoughts and vibrations. And they have naturally attuned themselves to the dark realms. Their vibrations haven't been merely produced by circumstances and conditions on earth. They have rather chosen such vibrations and patterns themselves.

How can they be helped if they can't attune to other spirits?

It's like a fog all around. When you're in the fog the fog is all around you. You cannot see very far at all. But, if someone brings a strong light before you, if someone brings a torch, a light can shine through the fog and so it is with those in the darker regions, with those trying to reach them with these lights. And if they can receive that light they will gain sight and recognition, which will mean a turning around of their souls. But they must be ready. Sometimes they must experience life in the dark realms and grow tired of it and grow to know that something else must exist, something better. They might also grow to know that they might be part of the problem, that they are the problem. Therefore, the germ of change is born and they can then be more receptive to life.

How can they help themselves after that?

They have to reach out. Help is always available for those who are humble and reach out. Those who seek help will receive it. It is a law. Once they've responded to the light, the bridge is created, the mould is broken and there's hope of movement, of change. They may need to spend some time yet in the darker realms, but they are on their way, they have broken the mould and it is only a matter of time before they will move on. It is a source of sadness to us all that there are those in the darker realms and we will endlessly strive to reach out to bring them back to the communal soul.

*   *   *

The following is the medium's (Paul) account of an experience with a spirit who had recently passed over in circumstances of war:

*   *   *

One night I experienced an energy that was at once sad, confused, a dawning of having lived in a delusion while on the earth plane. The being found himself in a reality in the spirit world that was at great odds with his vision of what his circumstances and status would be from the vantage point of his earthly life. The pain of discovering that both his vision of his earthly life and his spiritual destiny immediately after death were delusional was almost overwhelming. Both visions, which of course were interwoven, had led to courses of action that the spirit was now forced, into re-evaluating which was itself a painful process.

All of this was conveyed in a fleeting instant in what was predominantly a stream of feeling. It was also as if the being found himself surrounded by a fog and felt isolated and alone. Yet in one small part of this fog a brilliant small light strove to break through. There was thus hope in this situation and we were told that spirit guides had indeed recently reached the spirit and this was why we were able to have some communication with him.

It was the first time that I'd experienced this kind of energy with its feelings of sadness, solitariness, and pain. I was aware of almost a sense of betrayal yet there was no betrayer only the person's own delusions had betrayed him. Both the nature of the energy and its feelings and the surprise to me initially made it difficult to let go and allow the spirit to communicate. His response to this hesitancy was agitation, impatience and frustration with me; again a new experience, which I had not had before in channelling any other spirit communicator.

*   *   *

A few months later the same spirit made another unscheduled visit. One member of the group asked:

How are you now?
Not well, not well.
Are your guides still close to you?
They try; they try. But pain—too good (referring to guides)—not clear—pain repeated, constantly. They try; they try.
Is it very hard?
It is hard; it's hard. The prison of the mind is more secure than the stone walls of your prisons on earth. The prison of your mind is more powerful, stronger than the prisons of earth.
You are still getting help?
They reach to me, the Good Ones. But it presses in on me.
Is there anything we can do to help you?
You can reach out to me. Reach out with the Good Ones.
We do send the healing to you.
Thank you, thank you.
And we send it to the world leaders as well.
They must learn to talk. Must learn to reach out with their hearts not their guns. You reach out to world leaders with your hearts, your loving thoughts. Connect, link with the Good Ones to help them in their work.
Have you been able to meet up with anyone from your family since you've been in the spirit world?
Lonely, lonely, but I feel the warmth of the Good Ones, those who are all forgiving. I feel the pain of their "all forgiving."
Does that actually make you feel worse?
Humiliated, humbled for I was not all forgiving.
We don't know what we may have done in other lives. We only know the way we are now.

No, I know. I will go now. Please pray for me. Please pray for me, all of you.

Yes we will all pray for you.

You have kind hearts. You have kind hearts.

Thank you for coming. I wish we could take the pain away for you.

Your love takes the pain away. Your love takes the pain away.

*   *   *

WB came through immediately after to explain what had happened. It would appear that the spirit group were concerned in case the visitor had disturbed any of us. He explained:

Yes. Well that was an extremely sudden experience for you. It occurred by chance. It occurred by chance, you understand. There was a connection between the medium and this person and the connection fused like an electric spark. It is like you know, if you put two electrical sources close to each other then suddenly you make a spark, a connection, you understand. This is what we had here.

Had Paul been thinking about him?

No, it was totally by chance. You connect, as you know with many, many souls when you sit like this. You have many around you all the time and it may be that some of you connect with certain individuals, on occasions, at certain times but they would generally not have the need to make their presence more firmly felt. But this soul had a need to use the opportunity to connect with you and by doing so, you aided him greatly along with the other workers who work with him to help, so you have done him a great service this night.

He's been before, hasn't he?

Yes and because of that he's found it easy to connect with you once more. As you know it's more difficult if you haven't known the person but you've connected with this one before so once a connection always a connection, I fear in some ways, but you have rendered this soul a great service this evening, all of you.

How does it help him, WB?

It helps him because he feels your love and your concern. He feels your interest and because he's come to the conclusion that he's of no interest, and is not worthy of interest, or concern because of his actions, which he has difficulty in reconciling himself with now that he's achieved a different perspective on things. But by offering him love both from the spiritual worlds and from your earthly world you're rendering him a great service. For love truly heals all in time. For if souls feel your love they *know* it, they *feel* it, they *sense* it. They know it's not sham, they know it's not contrived or false. Therefore it's much stronger than words. Words may convey love, the soul can *feel* your love, and therefore they know it's not sham, but genuine.

One member of the group indicated that the visitor had startled her. Jacob responded:

I am sorry if this startled you. It's a rare occasion you understand Janet, a rare occasion, but it can happen on occasion. He (referring to Paul) was rather hoping for Davia to come through to lighten and contrast with what had gone before but we decided that I'd come through to provide an explanation and, (laughs) to confound his expectations.

Chapter 4

Communications from Angels

From time to time, we've received communications from angels. Our most regular angelic visitor introduced her/himself as Zeon. One of the communications is transcribed below. It's followed by a question prompted by the visit, with Hai's response.

Zeon told us:

We love you all dearly. We cannot express with words the love, which we shower on you. You must never doubt your sanctity. You must never doubt your worth, because you are worth more than your words can describe, each and every one of you. You are deserving of love from all in deepest measure.

How did you become an angel?

You don't become an angel. You are an angel.

Will you always be an angel?

I will always be an angel for the foreseeable future in eternity. But we may evolve just as you evolve because we share the same spiritual life, the same spiritual evolution. We are all of the One Mind and manifest in different forms, different expressions of Its Consciousness.

Do you have wings?

We manifest as befits the person who perceives us. We manifest in such a way that they can access us, can perceive us so our appearance does not trouble them. We have an appearance, which they can relate to. But these wings and such things are mere symbols and have nothing to do with our reality.

How would you appear to a fellow angel?

We are beings of light. Beings of light, is the best we can do to express a more fundamental representation of Reality but you also are beings of light. We share in the light, which is the Universal Creation.

What kind of work do you do?

We know what we must do. We know what we must do just as you get up in the morning to start your day. It is natural to us. We know what we must do. We know our calling and our mission.

Do you exist in the Everlasting Now or do you exist in a different time?

You exist in the Everlasting Now. We no more exist in the Everlasting Now as you yourselves do; it is only the appearance of relativity, which makes you think otherwise. The very presence and perception of duality is only possible because of the Everlasting Now, which is its source and its foundation.

You sound extremely knowledgeable. Is it instinctive to you or do you go to be trained in some way?

We are close to the Fabric of Reality.

I cannot understand what you mean. Can you explain more?

You have been told to look within by Hai. If you do so you will find the Fabric of Reality.

Is this in some way linked to the Stillness that Hai talks about?

The Stillness; Fabric of Reality, One Mind, Essence, or God. All these are words and concepts, which will ensnare you if you allow them to. Before a word is spoken, what are you? But I usurp Hai's place in speaking of such matters.

It's nice to get a second opinion.

The second opinion, my dear friend, is as the first. When the time is ripe you will see the simplicity of what we try to convey to you in all its glory.

I'll look forward to that.

Don't look forward, or you will forever be looking forward for something that is yet to come. And yet it is already with you, my friend. It is already with you in all its glory.

So, although it's all thought—provoking, it shouldn't be?

Thoughts are not the Divine Essence. The Divine Essence makes thoughts possible. Before thought occurs, there is the Divine Essence. What is it? I don't expect an answer!

Do we each have an angel?

We are commissioned to care for you, to be friends to you, to do what we can to guide you on your way.

Do we each have one angel?

You do not need one-to-one. Suffice to say that you have angel friends around you.

Do you mean there is one for every household or for every family?

An angel is a being of diverse qualities. There's no need to attach one angel to one person, but you are not short of the love of us. You are not short of help and assistance when you need it. The love we give out is deep and rich and in abundance for all.

So your capabilities as an angel allow you to administer to anyone?

Just so: People have thought of us as gods in some cultures. We are not gods. We are spiritual beings. But we have diverse qualities and abilities, which we use to be of benefit and help to others. We reach out with our love and those who have the hearts and the eyes to see may see, may feel our love. But the times do not facilitate this. People are more distracted these days than was formerly the case. But for those who have patience, who have love in their hearts and reach out to us, they may perceive us, and feel our reaching out of love.

Is it possible that some may mistake you for a guide?

It's possible. We work alongside your guides and there's a degree of overlap of roles, but we work together, we blend together in our activity on your behalf.

Is a guide's job a one-to-one job?

This is more the case, but, even so, a guide for you might also be a guide for someone else. You all must not think too particular. You are all individual human beings, individual souls and it is natural for you to wish for someone special who relates solely to you. But as you evolve, grow, and develop, you will realise that the depth and abundance of love that we have doesn't short measure you merely because we are also helping others. The fact that we do so doesn't diminish the depth of the love that we have for you as an individual being. Love is as fathomless as the depths of the deepest ocean. It's without bounds. It cannot be used up or exhausted. It's an ever-flowing river.

You have given us more things to think about.

Do not think too much. *Feel* it in your hearts.

That gives to me an indication of the depth of love that you actually feel for us all.

We are also, remember, expressions of the One Mind, the One Reality and if you truly wish to dip your heart into this One Mind of Reality you would be best to be aware that the Ground of all Being, all Existence is like a fathomless Heart. It's not an abstract concept. It is a fathomless, all-embracing Heart.

Does the One Mind develop and evolve?

The One Mind cannot develop or evolve in that **it is**, always has been, and always will be. It contains the seeds of all possibilities. It expresses itself through its creation, through its manifestation and discovers itself, if you like, but it cannot evolve because—**It is, the might be**. It's the might be of all possibilities and all possibilities are already within it.

Do you have free will?

We do have free will. It is the way we discover ourselves, our identity with the One Mind.

It was time for Zeon to leave and he gave us his blessing:

*　　　　　　　*　　　　　　　*

I must leave you now, but I wish you a fond farewell and remember our love. Remember the love that we all share amongst ourselves as spiritual beings. Try to love each other with the depth of love, which we all are worthy of, even in your difficult physical circumstances. I will go and bid you farewell and we may speak again perhaps, sometime in the future,—your future. Goodbye.

*　　　　　　　*　　　　　　　*

A few weeks later Zeon paid us a second visit. He began the conversation by telling us:

Show wisdom in your lives and in your decisions. Be free souls, free souls to fly to the heights of the light on the wings of your courage and hope. I am not used to your words so you must bear with me but I am pleased to spend time again with you.

What language do you normally speak in Zeon?

We do not need language. Our minds can link direct, can fuse together to convey in perfection our thoughts and feelings and only because we have reached a level which is closer to the Essence are we able to do this. If you were able on your plane to fuse your minds in this way it would cause you all manner of difficulties because your emotions and thoughts are mixed, do as you will to purify them. But you work on your plane to purify them and you will evolve to a state where you also may fuse your minds in harmony and divine communion and companionship.

Is that our destiny then?

Your destiny is that what you are now.

Is it very difficult when people pass over because they will still be the same as when on earth, won't they?

They truly are the same as they are here and therefore, there are the problems with which you associate with the earth life; so there are indeed problems. But the path is ever onward and as we go along the path our emotions are purified, our intent is purified and develops its harmony with others.

Does it cause difficulties and create disharmony to start with, if newly arrived spirits cannot keep their thoughts to themselves?

There are natural safeguards built in to assist with this evolution so the problems are not so serious. You evolve and as you evolve you move on and when the time is right you are able to link more with the minds of others.

Is it a very speedy form of communication?

It is instantaneous; distance knows no obstacle. It is like with your primitive communication systems where you know the right code you can talk to someone on the far side of the ocean; it is like that with us also but we know the direct code to the other persons mind. We reach out and we naturally find them and they respond.

The same person, a medium, continued:

I "received" some philosophy whilst sitting in church, which said; "all the wisdom you could find is inside you." Can you comment on that?

Has Hai not already told you of this? The One Mind is within and without. It embraces all, It runs through all; It **is** all. It is the Essence. It is all that can ever be; It is all wisdom that can ever be. If you reach within you tap into it and you have oceans of wisdom at your disposal.

Does this Essence you talk of actually come from our spirit or our soul?

There is no distinction; there is an At-Onement. But if you explore the "swamp" you project this wisdom outside of yourself whereas, **it resides within**. We say the same things to you all in a thousand different ways to enable understanding.

Yes, I can understand that what suits one will not suit another, will it?

And what suits you one night will not suit you another night.

Are we that complicated?

Truly: You make yourselves that complicated. But we do not say this by way of blaming. It is the state of things. It is the natural order. It is inevitable. But we must reach with simplicity with simple hearts and all will be revealed.

Is it just the work of our conscious minds, which makes us complicated?

Your conscious minds are necessary because your conscious minds create the world that you see around you as much as any objective reality. You cannot do without your conscious minds for they have their part to play in creating the world in which you live.

Do you have a conscious mind in spirit?

We are sentient, we have consciousness, but the consciousness of which I speak is of a different order, a different vibration to the consciousness that you have on your earthly journey.

Someone else asked:

Are the books written about angels accurate?

People elaborate and embellish our existence. It does not matter too much if the images they create help them on their way, but they do embellish, exaggerate and embroider our presence, our form and our existence, but it is of no deep consequence; there are far more fundamental things which are of consequence.

Did you develop into an angel through the earthly ways or were you always an angel?

This was a similar question to the one asked on Zeon's first visit. However, this time Zeon expanded on his reply. He told us:

We are a different pattern of evolution. We are spiritual first and foremost, as you are spiritual, but we have not taken the earthly path as a way of development. Our way is a different way to the earth people; it has its own challenges and its own responsibilities.

Do you start as fairies, or is that another separate evolution?

We are another pattern; there are many patterns in our Father's houses.

Is an angel very busy?

We are busy in a way that would not be understandable to you; we are busy in our own way.

Do you have time to talk to other angels, for instance, do you have a community where you meet?

We *are* a community. We have no need of meeting for we are a community; we are at Onement with each other.

I must leave you now—but I go to remain near. Goodbye my *spirit* friends.

*   *   *

One night Eileen asked Hai a question about angels. This prompted another visit from Zeon.

Eileen asked:

If by coming to earth we form our personality, how do Angels and nature spirits form their personality if they don't come to earth?

Hai quickly left and within seconds Zeon had arrived to answer the question for him. He told us:

We are of a different order, a different state of being. We operate and live in a different environment, a different dimension. The tools we need for development are different and are varied according to our *being* and our needs. But even so we share a spiritual essence with you all. We feel emotion more keenly, more refined. We are beings of emotion but not of the emotion in the way that you are accustomed. We have a keen sense of feeling; our being is *feeling* of a refined nature. We reach out with this *being* with great love. We are selfless beings yet should our selflessness become distorted, become tainted this selflessness becomes a selfishness beyond measure.

Questions about Angels

On another occasion, a member of the group put the following questions to Hai, about Zeon and angels in general:

I noticed the other night, when Zeon came through, that there was a significant difference in Paul's voice.

Zeon affects the energy, being the consciousness which Zeon projects. He's a great and loving being. He has to use the human voice as he finds it. He has to adapt, translate his intent, his message, into the human voice form.

Is it possible to have more than one guardian angel assigned to one person?

No. Generally the angels will look over a number of people because they are advanced beings and they have the capability to look over more than one person. So, although we can talk of having a guardian angel, the guardian angel whose business it is to look after us will also look after others.

I read a report of an angel lifting someone up in order to save her from being hit by a car. Could this happen?

Yes, this can happen. You will find other stories like this.

Do angels have sexuality?

No. No male or female exists when it comes to angels. Angels are angels. They are allocated gender as a convenience. Gender isn't important, or relevant to the angel. Angels are higher spiritual beings. Gender doesn't apply but they may use gender or people may perceive them as having gender but this is to do with making them more accessible to you.

Are angels allocated to us from the moment we are incarnated into this physical life and do they stay with us until we go back to the spirit world or do they change as we go through the physical life?

Your angels stay with you but other angels may also become involved with your development.

Are angels larger than us?

Hai laughs and responds:

Larger than life, yes.

Do they look like us?

They are beings of light. They can manifest as they see fit in many different ways but they are beings of light. It is their intrinsic nature, which is more important than how they manifest their appearance for their appearance is versatile according to their wish and your need; therefore, they have no fixed form or appearance.

So if we sense a loving spirit around us, we probably wouldn't know whether it was an angel?

You may know but it is not always certain that you can tell. But what does it matter? If you can be aware of a loving person around you then surely this is what is important.

Do people sometimes receive white feathers as evidence of spirits/angels?

This can happen but it does not mean it happens all the time. But yes, it is an apport. (Spirit gift)

Do spirits have guardian angels?

No. The community of souls is ever aware of our needs, ever responsive to our needs. In the spirit lands we are never left to our own devices.

*   *   *

Zeon has visited us on a number of occasions. Each time we feel we are in the presence of a being of great love and wisdom. Throughout our experience of speaking with spirits, we find periods when we almost seem to slide into a routine and perhaps almost become a little blasé. It is often then that the spirits will deliberately vary their contact, perhaps to shake us out of our rut and give us something to think about. We were just getting used to the idea of talking to angels when we received one of these "shake ups" in the form of a different kind of angelic visit:

The Group Spirit Angel

The Angel told us:

I am connected to you all, but not because of a life on the earth plane. I am of angelic being. I am the spirit, which has been attached to your group, your angelic being. I sit in the empty chair. I'm the spirit of your group. I am the spirit for you and when you are not together I'm aware of your presence; you are linked through me. I am like the soul of the group. I'm like its heart. I am of angelic essence. I have a role in the harmony of your group and in it's heart. And when you are not together, the heart still exists.

The idea of an angel being attached to the group generated a number of questions. One of our group started the questions flowing:

Did you choose to join us or was it the other way round?

There was a coming together, a mutuality. You may think of me as the Guardian Angel if this helps you to understand. When you are apart, you are still together. You may think of me as "the simple voice."

If anyone else joined the group, would it be affected?

You may bring others in if you wish. If you feel that they would be able to join your harmony, you may add others and welcome them in. There are others who could join, but you must seek them out and be sure that they are of like mind and heart.

When you talk of influencing the harmony of the group, does this influence the energies?

Yes, it does indeed. It influences the energies for all manner of things of the spiritual.

Do you work with everybody else in the Spirit Group?

We work closely together.

Is your role's different to Zeon's?

Yes. I'm specially allocated to work with your group. I link to the soul of your group; you create a heart from your separate hearts.

It almost sounds as though the group has got a soul of its own then?

You create a unity with your love.

The empty chair you spoke of earlier. Is that symbolic?

Our Angel friend didn't answer this question directly. Instead he replied:

I am tangible yet intangible, real yet apparently intangible. I am a being of brilliant white light.

I associate knowledge with white light.

I have knowledge in plenty and I give of what I have. But the knowledge that I give is the knowledge that exists before words are thought of. I leave you now. I leave you with my blessing. You know that I am not far away.

Chapter 5

Guides

Guides

We've had many discussions with Hai, Paul's principal guide, about the role of guides. However, we've also had discussions with various other guides as well. Two of Eileen's guides have communicated on a regular basis and have indicated that their role is to help her with spiritual healing. Red Cloud lived his last incarnation in the 19th century as a North American Indian. He presents as a very strong, authoritative character. Patience tells us she was one of the early Quaker settlers in North America. She presents as a gentle, patient person and has explained that her role is to facilitate the easy flow of the energy in healing.

One of the points of interest to visitors has been the backgrounds of guides and whether there are any common characteristics. Hai was asked:

Why are most of the guides Red Indians?

Hai smiled and responded:
I do not have any feathers! There are many spirit guides. They are not all, by any means, of Indian ancestry. There are some who, when on the earth plane, were North American Indian in identity, but many were not Indian. I think there is an element here of people being more sensitive, expectant about Indian guides because of the associations, which they create in relation to our Indian brothers. The range of guides is immense. It is perhaps the case, though, that those who are

prominent in undertaking this role, the role which I myself have taken, had a particular orientation while on the earth plane and this predisposes or enables us more easily to step into the role we occupy. This perhaps relates to the fact that your conditions of life distract people from advancing in certain directions, detract and distract them from developing certain affinities and skills. So it may be that some cultures better prepare people for the role, even into the afterlife in the spirit land.

Why would a guide choose to be a guide and come to the earth plane to speak through a medium?

Well, they would choose to be a guide because of their love for the people. They would choose out of their love of those who still walk the earth in tribulation and trouble, which those who become guides may become identified with, because they also have walked the earth, in trial and tribulation. And therefore, when they see the tribulations of those of you who still walk the earth, they open their hearts in compassion to your need, to your silent call, the call that you yourselves are not always aware of. But you *do* send out a call from your troubled hearts and we answer as best we may. Not because we are privileged beings. Not because we are above you in any sense of the word but because we are your brothers, your sisters, in love. This is why we answer your call. This is why we try to meet your need.

Someone else asked:

What do guides do? Do they influence us?

They influence you Katherine they try to shape, to affect your thoughts in the nicest possible way. They try to encourage you, to help you, to assist you. But they are dependent upon your motivation, your intent. They cannot override this, they can only respond to your intent, your drive. If you have positive intent, positive drive then they can work in tandem with you on this. They can respond to this positive drive and assist you with it but they cannot override your drives, your intents. Do you understand me? So if you reach out in a particular way they can help you with this if it is in accordance with the nature of things.

Do angels and guides have special tasks?

You have your guides and you have your angels. You have other spirits who also have an interest in your welfare, being and development. All these spirits have a role to play. You should not become too preoccupied with the different roles of the different spirits, for they all have their place and they all work in harmony for your greater good. Also their roles may change over time to suit the needs of the occasion, to suit the needs of your development, of the times, which you go through at different stages of your life. Things may change, they are not fixed, they are fluid but fluid for the benefit of yourselves.

Are there special occasions when they all join in together to help us?

They all join together all the time. We are aware of each other's efforts and we work in harmony for your greater good. What is more important is that you join to us, that you *consciously* join to us. We will do what we can from our side but this is greatly assisted by your reaching out to us in harmony and love, working with us. We do not impose anything on you. We do not seek to impose anything on you, for your life is sacred to yourselves and your life is a matter for you. You make your own decisions. You have your own free will. This is sacrosanct to us that you have your own free will and you must use this free will wisely, but even used unwisely you learn lessons and you grow and develop through the exercise of your free will. We work with you; we work with your free will, for your development.

If we asked for help it would be easier to thank the spirit if we knew who had given the help?

You have merely to reach out. You have merely to reach out with the intention of help, with the intention of wishing for help, with the intention of offering thanks to those who help you. You have a bond with us. You have a bond with all spirits who work with you. You do not need to know names; you do not need to know personalities, for we work with you closely, intimately and when you reach out with your intention, with your feelings of love, you touch us, you connect with us. Do not rely on words.

So how do they know how we appreciate them if we don't actually say thank you?

They know because you reach out to them. If you have the loving feeling within your heart, if you have the feeling of appreciation within your heart, if you have a feeling of love within your heart, you reach out to your guides, to your angels, to the spirits who seek to help you. They, therefore, know your appreciation and this is reward enough. We are not limited by your communications, by your modes of communication, for we can connect with your minds if you reach out to us. We will not impose our presence. We will not impose our thoughts and our wishes but if you reach out to us we are able to connect with you and your loving thoughts, your harmonious thoughts, connect with us. Our communication is more reliant on the *thought* and *emotion* than your communications in your earthly life. You communicate your emotions and thoughts through other mediums, through your language, through your word of mouth but we are not restricted to such communication forms. We are able to connect directly through mind, thought; through emotion, through love, through spiritual energy and therefore you reach us. You connect with us when you use your thoughts, when you use your emotions; you connect with us.

Are guides and angels taken for granted rather than thanked by most people on the earth plane then, Hai?

Most people are not aware of their guides or spirits but this a condition, which is more prevalent in your times perhaps because of society and times in which you live. People are not encouraged to imagine that there are spirit entities around them. They are not encouraged to imagine that they may work in association with spirit beings but such spirit beings are around, nevertheless, and willing and ready to work with people.

If we follow the advice of our guides, does it help the guides in their progress?

By offering yourselves to us in that we may help you, you help us, for as we give, so we receive. As we give, so we receive the opportunity to help ourselves.

Can guides choose the person they want to be a guide for?

We are mutually drawn to each other, because we all have our own predispositions. We all have our own common interests. We all have our own affinities and these affinities are like magnets, which pull people together. I was pulled to Paul because of his affinity with the religion of my times when I was an Abbot, a Zen Abbot. We were pulled together through this affinity like magnets and indeed we had a common affinity because of a shared past life also.

Do you know who your spirit guide was when you were on this earth plane, Hai?

Yes.

Are you allowed to tell us who it was?

He was a great teacher with a desire for my progress.

Is it possible for someone like me to be a guide for other people eventually?

All people may become guides ultimately. When the period, when the stage of development is reached, we may all become guides with the advancement of wisdom, with the development of our inner self. But the time before this happens for some may be great; the time for others may be small.

Are there different levels of spirit guides like, for instance, one to four?

Hai laughs and replies:

Or one to four hundred. (Laughter) We would not encourage you to think in numbers or levels and grades. This is not helpful ultimately. Suffice it to say that you have the guide that is appropriate to you, who is a "good fit" for you at the moment.

Is it possible for your own spirit guide to be with you all through your life?

This may be the case sometimes. At other times it is necessary for the spirit guide to move on so that others may come to you and work with you. The fundamental purpose of your guide is to assist you in your unfoldment and development, to guide you in this, to hold your hand in this as an equal partner in it. A guide should not be viewed as someone to lead you by the hand but rather you walk side by side, hand in hand; you follow me? So this is the way you should see your guide, not as someone who is one step ahead pulling you along by the hand. You may find that your guide may change over time, but it is *your* need, which dictates what shall happen and nothing else.

Do our guides ever get fed up with us?

No, No, Janet, they do not get fed up, they have a love for you, a love of your heart.

Do you have to report back to anyone "above" you regarding the progress you are making, bearing in mind what you said previously?

You mean reporting back to the "big chief?" (Laughter) No not as such. We work together with others. We converse with others; we may consult with others but there is no bureaucracy, no.

*   *   *

On another occasion, one member of the group had been reading about "higher" guides and asked Hai the following:

Who are the Ascendant Masters, Hai?

Ascendant masters have evolved to a high plane spiritually and who, nevertheless, because of their love for human kind and other spirits, are prepared to relinquish some of their privileged status, privileged environment, in order to teach, in order to communicate, in order to commune with those on other planes.

Do they communicate with one person or with many?

They communicate with many, at different times, at the same time. You must not, as I have said, become too attached to the idea of Ascendant Masters, Descendant Masters, and so on, for there is only the One Reality and we are part of that One Reality. In the same way names of guides are not important. You must listen to the truth that you hear and ask yourselves: Is it the truth? You must listen with your hearts as well as your minds and ask yourselves: Does this ring true? Does this strike a chord in my heart? Does this stand the test? There are those who would have you follow so and so, such and such a person. Such and such a person has the most truth. Such and such a person has more truth than so and so, and so on. You see my point? You must work out for yourself the truth, which is all around us. You must divine the truth for yourself. All these people, myself included, can give you pointers, food for thought, spiritual food, but you must eat the fruit yourself to know its essence. Do not become a follower for the sake of becoming a follower, because you yourself must become the teacher.

So an open mind is the best?

Open mind with no attachment to yourself, to the implications for yourself. Open mind free of ego.

You told us a while ago that you had a lot of information about us. That you knew a lot about us. How do you get that information?

We get this information by observing you all, through our links with spirit also. We have many sources of information (smiles) to build up a dossier on you. We do not use this in an inappropriate way, however, as sometimes happens on your earth. Our intent is honourable.

Healing Guides

Red Cloud on one of his visits to the circle had the following to say:

I sat with the white men you know, to try and make peace, but they did not want peace. They wanted peace on their terms and not to take account of our needs, of our traditions, of our heritage. This was a sad thing.
Did you think you had made peace with the white man?
We thought we would be able to, but they did not want it. They wanted our lands. They wanted their own way. The land belongs to no one and everyone. Land should not be fenced and parcelled out.

As Red Cloud works through Eileen in her healing work, a circle member, who was particularly interested in spiritual healing, had the following questions for him:

Do you have an interest in healing any particular illness?
Only those conditions that bring ill health. I wish to correct them, to put them right, to relieve the pain and suffering of those who need it, in mind and body.

The same group member, who is particularly sensitive to the spirit energies, had indicated on a previous occasion that the immensity of Red Cloud's presence and energy had slightly unnerved him. Red Cloud, aware of the person's comments, tried to reassure him. He told him:

I do not mean to be intimidating. I just bring my power to your circle. (Smiles) I have got my tomahawk in my belt, so it is no threat to you.
I'm very pleased.
It is at home in my belt.
So you do not need it?
Save to cut the knots that bind, which are many, but they dissolve.
How are you, Red Cloud?
I am in excellent health, which befits a healer.

Eileen, always keen to know that the healing works well, asked the following:

Is the healing doing all right?
The healing does well, but some healers must heal themselves to do better. When there was trouble in my tribe, when there was trouble created by the young ones, the elders brought them together to talk sense to them. To make them see sense. But you must have a wise elder to achieve this.

*   *   *

Patience

One night another of Eileen's guides, Patience, communicated. She told us that in her last incarnation she was a Quaker and had emigrated to America in the 1700s. When asked, she explained that she is no longer with her husband but that it does not matter because not all relationships formed on earth are meant to last.

After offering us some detail about her life, the following personal discussion took place.

Eileen asked:
Do you have a particular role with the healing?
I have the role of clearing the path, Eileen, of making things straight and level.
Is that in all matters, or specifically healing?
In your matter of the healing, I assist and facilitate to help things progress well.
Have you known me since I got interested in the healing?
I have known you for some time before the healing.
Did you know that I would become interested in healing, then?
Yes, we knew of this.
How do you help smooth the way in healing?
My temperament helps to smooth the way, to overcome the "bumps."
Are there many bumps to iron out with my healing?
There are always bumps to iron out, but we progress. This is the important thing, is it not? We iron out the bumps. There may be more

along the way, but we iron them out. And so we go on and before we know where we are, we make rapid good progress, a bit at a time, one step at a time, a hill at a time, to climb the mountain.

What do the bumps refer to? Are they energies?

The bumps are blockages, inconsistencies. You must know yourself the difficulties, which we all face, from your side and ours. There are fluctuations in faith, more fluctuations in the channel and other fluctuations in how strong the contact may be between us. All of these things are bumps, are they not, blockages? We cannot hope to iron things out to become a level smooth plane, because our lives are not like that. Inevitably there will always be bumps to be ironed out, but we may progress, nevertheless, and the bumps may get fewer and not as big.

Another circle member asked:

If you were living today, do you think you would be drawn towards the hospitals?

I am drawn to caring, yes.

Do you work exclusively with Eileen?

I do not work exclusively, but we have a special bond.

*   *   *

Over time, there has, been a fair amount of ritual and belief developed over healing. Hai, Red Cloud, and Patience have always said that ritual is not necessary, or desirable for effective healing. In fact, Red Cloud has humorously said that he would like to take his tomahawk to all ritual. Nevertheless, Eileen still asked Patience whether it mattered if some of the ritual was forgotten.

When channelling healing the other night, I forgot to do certain things. Will it matter?

You should not worry and you should not worry about doing things in a particular way. So you speak of your rituals and you succumb to them again.

Can anybody act as a healing channel?

There is great potential for many to be healing channels, if you wish to serve, if you wish to act as a channel. It is a seeking, a reaching out in love, which is the most important thing. We cannot over-emphasise to you, that love is the ground of all things, the foundation, the essence of all things, and no matter how often we say this; we need to keep saying it, because people again make what is simple, complicated.

Absent Healing

Patience was asked:
What is the best way to send absent healing?
She replied with amusement:
Absently, yes, absently—how else can you send absent healing but absently?

We all laughed. Patience continued:

You need to simply remind yourself of the person and direct your thoughts to them, your loving thoughts to them.
Do you need to imagine them fit and well?
Just imagine them. Just imagine them with loving thought healing loving thoughts going out to them. Do not worry about technique again.
How often should I do this?
You are still on technique. You should remind yourself of them as reminiscence comes. You should remind yourself of them and you may then direct your thoughts spontaneously, naturally.
Are you saying, then, that absent healing is just a natural process?
It is a natural process. You send your thoughts out to them and they will respond, their body will respond, their minds will respond to your healing thoughts.
What about people you don't know but whom someone has asked for healing?
You send out your thoughts to them. You have some anchor point, you have some point of recognition of the person whom you are thinking of; a name, a thought, so you use whatever anchor point you have to focus on the person and send them your loving thoughts.
Is it necessary to ask someone to send the healing energy?
If you send out your loving healing thoughts; such entities who are concerned with such things will facilitate your intent, will aid your

enterprise. It is the loving thoughts that you send out which act as a broadcast beacon and they direct themselves to the person you have in thought. It is automatic.

*   *   *

It is our practice, at the end of every sitting, to send out the energy to those who've requested healing and for world peace. One of our circle members decided to check out with Hai that it was actually having the desired affect. He asked:

When we send out the energy after our sittings, does that work?

Hai responded:

It is as if the person were in the room with you. Send your thoughts out. Those thoughts connect. Those loving healing thoughts connect in ways in which you do not appreciate, with a depth you do not appreciate.

So, if we sent out the healing in a general way to all the people in the world who need it most.

Yes, your loving thoughts are translated into benevolent actions.

And does it go to the most needy?

It goes to the needy. You do not have to worry about the *most* needy, the deserving needy, or the most deserving needy. You do not have to concern yourself with those things. All you have to do is send out your loving thoughts. The One Mind is greater than you know. You do not need to accept responsibility or try to take responsibility for apportioning need and help, for making judgements about who is most needy. You simply need to follow your hearts and send out your loving thoughts.

Chapter 6

More Questions

The first three questions are not directly related to the spirit world. It nevertheless seemed appropriate to include them here.

Hai was asked:

So will the earth always exist in its present form?
I do not say that, because the earth moves towards its own evolution. As humanity evolves, and a greater balance is achieved between the physical and the spiritual, a greater harmony, so the realisation of the Common Unity, the Common Soul, will come more to the fore and people will be able to embrace each other more fully.

Was there ever a time when the earth was more in harmony than it is at present?
A sense of harmony has fluctuated over the ages, but there has never been the sense of harmony on earth to which I have just referred. It has shifted relatively, but it has not achieved the maturity, the beauty, and the fullness of which I speak.

What about Atlantis? Were those people no more in harmony than we on earth now?
No. They had their own good points and their own not so good points and it has ever been the way.

What sort of scale is the spirit world in relation to the earth?
It is vast! It is vast!

When people are born disabled, can they choose to be different when they return to the spirit world?

Of course they can, yes. Their disability is a temporary thing; a temporary thing, sometimes willingly taken on for the benefit of all, for the learning of all. And so my friends we must see beneath the transitory show. We must see beneath the transitory appearances before our eyes. We must see beneath all this my friends to the Eternal Beauty, the Eternal Love.

So do they choose to be how they would have been if they had not been born deformed?

They have never been deformed. They have never been deformed; they have been perfect in spirit.

So in spirit everyone is perfect?

Yes, but they present this disabled body to the world that the world may respond, that the world may be tested, its sight may be tested, yes.

Some people choose to come here that way, don't they?

This is true, to give test.

Not all choose though do they?

No but many times they do choose, to give test to the world.

They must be very brave.

Yes this is true. This is true.

*   *   *

One member of the group was concerned about an uncle who is now in the spirit world. She asked:

My uncle lost both legs with diabetes. He was always very cheerful in spite of this. Would he have known this before he was born and would he have chosen the disability?

Hai appeared to be in contact with the uncle when he replied. He told her:

He says; he knew the outcome of his life. A brave soul as you say. Yes, this shows to the world that you can still be positive, cheerful, in spite of affliction. This is of hope to the world.

On another occasion Hai was asked:

When people want to do things in the spirit world, do they just think of something and is it created for them?

It requires some organisation, but possibilities do exist for creating all manner of things.

Someone else asked another question:

Why don't the spirit world just let us get on with it when we come to the earth plane.

Although we come on this earth to undergo experiences we are not alone and it was never intended that we should be alone in our quest, in our venture. Therefore, there are those from the spirit plane as there are those on the earthly plane who accompany you on your journey, who help you, who are there to lend a hand. This is the nature of life; we are not alone. There are those around us who can help us whether on the earth or whether in the spirit, this is natural and is part of our life.

Is there anything at all that may be better on earth than on the spirit plane? I ask because I wonder why people rush to come back?

They come to gain experience as we have spoken before but there is a beauty in itself of the love that we can show each other on the earth plane in spite of all the adversity, of the conditions of life, which we have to live through. There is a depth of love, which can be shown, that enriches our ability to love, which refines our ability to love and this we carry forward with us into the spirit planes.

Is it not possible to achieve that in the spirit plane, to the same extent?

It is perhaps too easy for us in some ways in the spirit planes. There the circumstances of life are not adverse in the way they are here. We can more easily show love to those around us because we are not submitted to the pressures and adversities which you are subjected to generally, though we can show our love deeply, we can reach out to those whom need help; to those in the darker regions especially who need our help. We who are on the more harmonious planes are not subjected to the same pressures and stresses that you experience.

Once we've have adapted to not being able to eat, drink, smoke, etc. Is there anything else we would miss?

Earth is like a second home and so in some ways as we would always have fond memories, fond associations, and all the natural feelings for a second home that we have left behind. So we have feelings for earth and the ways of earth. But it is no more than this and we may act out our feelings for our second home by coming to work with people like yourselves to whom we convey our love and affection knowing our common brotherhood, and the way of life which we have experienced on the earth plane, which we share and the deeper life which we share in spirit.

I have read a book that refers to, "The Community Of Souls." Can you tell us a little about them please?

The term "the community of souls," is just the feeling of community amongst the spirits who live in the spirits lands. There is no sense of isolation, we are ever in each other's thoughts, and there is a loving concern for everyone so there is a caring that goes on indefinitely.

Language

Is there a universal language in spirit?

Yes, you could say that, in that it is a language of thought, or rather ideas and feeling, emotion, richness beyond your wildest imaginations.

So we will be able to communicate with anyone?

By thought, yes.

Death

If people believed in spirit do you think it would ease bereavement when it comes to them?

Well, if people believe in spirit it is helpful at one level, is it not, for you can feel that the person is still in another dimension. Yet there is still the pain, the loss of separation in the *now* and there is a feeling still of loss and of distance; therefore, it does not solve the problem of bereavement. But if they were convinced of the truth of the reality of their loved one in the spirit world, this would assuredly assuage the pain, for they could look forward to the day when they could be reunited, even if they did not have this sense of presence now in the present time.

Spirit Pain

A member of the group had recently had a tooth removed. He asked Hai whether our spirit felt the pain of the physical body and how any operation or trauma affected it. Hai replied:

Well, when you have an operation your spirit is aware of the operation of course, but also it can put itself to one side of it, if you see what I mean. It can put itself to one side of physical pain, the pain of the operation. It is not the spirit, that is experiencing the pain but because of the close association of the spirit to your body, it feels the pain that your body feels, and so therefore, it participates in this pain. But in circumstances where pain is great, it may put itself to one side and withdraw, to an extent, from the source of this pain.

Near Death Experiences

When people have operations some say they left their body, others say it is a figment of their imagination. What does happen?

They may leave the body for a short time. They may put themselves on a sort of leash, if you like, by leaving the body, and they may look upon the body as if they are totally outside of it and in some sense they are totally outside of the body but they are still intricately connected with it.

Does this only happen if you actually die, or can it happen under anaesthetic?

You may leave your body in other circumstances also. If you travel outside of your body you look upon your body as if it is another person or entity. But yet you are still connected with your body and because you are still connected with your body you may return to it.

Would there be something to stop us visiting the spirit world in this situation?

You may visit spirit realms in this manner and still return to your body for it is like, as I said before, you are on a leash.

Does it work the opposite way, for example, can another spirit temporarily come into a physical body to experience what we are going through?

No. We may empathise with what they go through, we may associate with what they go through, we may sense, link and therefore understand what they go through but it is not like jumping into someone's body.

Soul Mates

One night one of our younger group members asked Isleen about soul mates. She replied:

There is no *one* soul mate as such; there are many souls that we come to love. We grow attached to many souls so you must not think of it as having one single soul mate whom we are bound to; there are a number. Love is broad and deep, broad and deep enough to have a number of souls who we can become close to, who we can feel we can be close to at your time of life. You are preoccupied, as others are of your age. Deep romantic relationships will come at their appointed time so do not overstress yourself about them. You have the whole of life in front of you.

Time of Passing

Someone asked Hai about information in a book they'd read. He said:

The book suggests that people pass over when they have learned all their lessons in life. Does this mean that someone who does not pass until, say 100 has only just learned the lessons?

Age is of no consequence; age has nothing to do with it, for there are lessons to be learned through a short life. The length of the life is neither here nor there in terms of the learning that may take place. It depends upon the needs of the person, it depends upon their karma, what they bring with them; it depends upon what their needs are. Some will come because indeed they need a long life, others may come knowing their life will be short but its value can be great still.

The Colour Black

Do you have the colour black in the spirit world?

The colour black is an unknown colour in the spirit world. Black is an absence of colour. We can of course create it if we so wish; we do not wish it. Why should we want to look at blackness when there is so much vibrant colour around us?

People on the earth who call themselves black often wish to promote the colour black.

If you look at black people they are not truly black at all. There is not a black face. Black is the absence of colour. The faces of the people on your earth are not black at all. They reflect the light to different degrees; there is no blackness there. Night is black. Blackness is the night; it is the absence of light. Black faces *reflect* the light. All people on the earth have different coloured skins. The difference in different coloured skins merely reflects the light in different ways. They are neither white nor black. Have you ever truly seen a white face? No, nor have I, except in the spirit lands where there are forms approaching white. But this is a matter of spirit not a matter of your form.

"Off Days" in the Spirit World

At the beginning of each sitting, it is customary for Hai to ask us if we are well. We always return the question—knowing what the answer will be. On one occasion someone asked if spirits had "off days" Hai replied:

We do not have "off days" as you do, no. We have our changes of mood, changes of emphasis but I would not say off days as such.

Part Two

Guest Speakers

Chapter 7

Rab: Billy: Black Beard

During our many hours of sitting we've had a great variety of spirits come through who don't belong to the spirit group who work with us. When one of our Circle members noticed the pattern of these visiting spirits, he named them "Guest Speakers." This quickly caught on and we now always refer to these spirits by that term.

The reasons why these spirits have come through to us have been equally varied. Some have been relatives and friends of Circle Members who wanted to re-establish contact and provide reassurance of their continued existence and interest in us. However, far more often we've received visits from spirits who have been totally unknown to us.

Very early on we started to realise that these were seldom random and that the visitors were being selected for a particular purpose. Often this was because on the earth plane they had a particular temperament or had specific experiences in one of their previous incarnations. We later understood that our Spirit Group was encouraging them to come through as it was felt that the spirits could usefully share these experiences to our benefit. Often our discussions with them also continued a theme, which we had discussed earlier with Hai or other members of our group and which complemented the answers that we'd received.

Some spirits visited us in response to events going on in the world at the time and they seemed to have a need to show that they empathised with our circumstances and feelings and to register their concern and support. Sometimes a link occurred between the current event and their previous lives on the earth plane. This was the case with one spirit visitor, who told us that he'd been a farmer in England at the time of Cromwell. He came through at the time of the outbreak of "foot and mouth" and showed great concern for the suffering of the animals and farmers.

The third category of visitor, are those who have some claim to fame of varying degrees. In the past I've seen various trance mediums working, and I have read many articles and books on the subject; nevertheless, I must admit to my more sceptical side coming to the fore when hearing of famous people communicating from the spirit world. I was no less sceptical in my own case, therefore, when some famous personalities started to emerge and for that reason I initially found the experience uncomfortable and disconcerting. However, it was subsequently explained to us that the bonds of love and affection are very powerful and because of our special affection for these spirits they were being drawn to us. Indeed, being aware of our love and without the constraints of the physical world to create barriers, the facility to establish contact was relatively straightforward.

Occasionally we've had spirits visit us, apparently "out of the blue," with no definite purpose other than they have affection for us, or an interest in our activities. We've been told on many occasions that, when we sit, it is as if we send out a beacon. This beacon attracts many spirits to our location who come, partly out of interest, but also to lend their energies to the enterprise. One night Hai was asked how The Phoenix Group chose our Guest Speakers: Below is what he said in reply.

*   *   *

You know we encourage various people to come to you, various people who are at various stages of development. So everyone who comes to your circle is not an enlightened soul, is not an, *all* good, soul. But they are souls who are "on the road," who seek the light, who seek the good, and even when we invite souls who are only on the first rungs of the ladder, they *are on* the first rungs of the ladder and are pointed in the right direction. We do not go dragging unwilling souls to you who are climbing down the ladder, who are on backward rungs of the ladder. We seek out souls for you who are climbing upward and even if they are on early rungs of the ladder they may have something of benefit to share with you; their experiences on this earthly plane or indeed from their experiences in the spirit realms. So we seek out spirits for this reason. But they are not all of the same level, not all of the same degree of evolvement, of understanding. Nevertheless, they can contribute in a worthwhile way to your endeavours.

And on another occasion Hai said a little more about the reasons for choosing our Guest Speakers:

There are many that we encourage to come through because they have a particular message that *they* are keen to transmit and therefore may be of benefit to you and others. They wish to share their experiences; they wish to express their compassion and concern for the earth and its people.

*   *   *

The following three Guest Speakers, Rab, Billy, and Black Beard all killed someone when last on the earth plane. These communications show, that it is not always that we have killed that determines our initial condition in the spirit world, but the circumstances and *feelings* that are present when the act is committed. You will notice that, in spite of the acts they committed, the humour the following communicators bring with them to demonstrate their point is not diluted.

Rab
The message: The power of Hate.

You need to get rid of your hatred and anger before coming over to the spirit world: That was the message our Scottish friend Rab had for us. He told us that he was alive at the time of Robert the Bruce and was involved in the fight against the English. He visited to develop discussion of a theme that comes up in our discussions on a regular basis—i.e. the theme of love and hatred.

Rab came through with a strong Scottish accent and the words and the way he said them have been transcribed (almost) verbatim. He told us:

Ye hate and ye hate gets a grip o'ye and ye cannot see it. Ye are so much taken up with it, it consumes ye. It drives ye and ye canna see it.

Ye are driven along by it. Ye hate and ye anger and ye canna turn ye self around because ye are driven. Ye are blind to what's happenin.' Ye are blind to it. Ye go along with yer hate and yer anger and yer hurtin. Ye hurt them, ye hurt others and ye canna see it; what's happenin.' And ye get so caught up in yer anger and yer hate that ye forget what it feels like to love and have compassion.

It's a sorry thing to happen and when you get here you've gotta unlearn it. And like I said, I met them lads (guides) over here who were as hard as steel. They would take no nonsense from me. They put me straight. Slowly, but surely, they put me straight. They didn't flinch. They didn't flinch from me, me rantin' and ravin.' They stood their ground like any warrior I'd come across. The best. And they worked with me and they nudged me slowly. And I relented and thought on what they'd said and I turned mesel around. Slowly turned mesel around. And eventually I was able to talk to some of those English lads whose skulls I'd split and we were able to become friends.

Aye! We get caught up in our causes. Get caught up in the flow. In the flows of the time we live, in the currents that buffet us around. We go with the current and get buffeted around. But we shouldna go with the current. We should make our own way. Make our own current.

*   *   *

A short while after, Rab paid us another visit. He elaborated a bit further:

Where did you find yourself when you passed over? Did you have loved ones come to meet you?
I had loved ones and I met some of those English. Met a few of those English lads, which I had put to rest. Not easy. Wasn't easy.
Did they forgive you? They must have been fighting too.
Ah, they were fightin,' but there wasn't always the hate there, wasn't always the hate in them. 'Cause they were following orders. We were fightin' our cause and we believed in the rightness of our cause. And in truth it was a right cause. But because we had a passion for our cause, that passion could bring on hate towards our enemies. And passion can turn into a fearful hate. So some of those English boys did

not suffer so much in the same way 'cause they were following orders. They shouldn't have followed them orders, but they did.

Did it take you a long time then to adjust?

It took me a while to settle, to calm me emotions. You gotta be careful about emotion over here. You bring powerful emotions over here, they ain't so easy to tame. They're a right handful. It's not so easy to calm them as it is here (earth). If you're riled up its not so easy to calm them.

So, were you still angry over there?

Right. I was still angry. I was angry. I was hateful.

When your anger started to fade, did your living conditions change? Did they improve?

Aye, lassie, because it creates harmony with your surroundins.' It means the vibration becomes more positive, more harmonious. And it means that this harmony can create more beauty, more peace, more congenial surroundins'.

Did you find yourself nearer to the darker regions when you first went over?

Aye, I was over that direction. Not in them regions themselves, but over that direction. Me hate was an honest hate, if you understand. There was no self in it. Not for mesel anyway. Though *any* hatred is some kind of self-importance.

That's not the same as being evil though, is it?

Ah, I bore no malice for *them*, but for what they did to us. For what they did to us and our families.

And did guides come and help you?

Aye, they came and helped. Aye, it felt more like a switchin.' Felt more like they were beatin' me bum raw. But that's because of the pain of adjustment, the pain of turning mesel around. It's painful.

Do you help other people now who are in a similar situation?

I help them who come over who have a grudge, who harbour hatred. I try to explain to them me own experience. How it does na pay. It does na pay to hang on to anger. Anger breeds anger and it goes in a big circle and never ends unless someone takes his claymore and breaks the circle. Breaks the circle of hate.

It must have been awful times for you?

Aye, awful times right enough. Awful times.

And do people listen when you tell them about your experience?

Yes, some of them do. Some of them listen. Some take a lot longer to listen. But I'm not on me own here and there's others who try to reach them too. Try to get through to them. This is the thing about hatred. You're so busy hatin,' ye canna hear what they're tryin to say. Stubborn, stubborn as a mule sometimes they are, like I was one time, stubborn as a mule. Those guides come and give them a switchin,' like they gave me a switchin,' a mental switchin.'

I suppose it must be difficult not to hate if you've had it passed down to you from parents?

Aye, it's more difficult. It's not easy to throw off if our parents have been up to mischief. It's more difficult to throw off. It wasna easy.

Someone commented on a book they'd read about contact with the darker realms of the spirit world. Rab responded:

You wouldn't go there for a holiday. You wouldn't go there for a day, never mind a holiday.

I've often thought I might be interested in that area of work.

Well, lassie, you see when you're there. Don't you go promisin' them anything.

OK. I'll wait and see.

Aye. You take the tour first. Davia (spirit stage manager) will give you the tour.

*   *   *

On Rab's third visit he was asked:

Do you still see the people you hated when on the earth plane?

Aye, they're still around. We're good friends now. I come and talk to ye the way I do to make a point, (Rab had started the original conversation with us by making derogatory remarks and jokes about the English) but we're good friends. We were just on the wrong side of the fence to each other. We were both driven by our situation, of the time. You have that now with your Irish. Driven by the situation at the time. Driven by the situation of the past. It's folly. It's like your concepts you were talking about with Hai before. Ye get ye concepts given to ye at birth and ye stick on to them and before ye know where ye are they've got ye all glued up. It's not sense. Waste, crying waste.

Do we have those concepts at birth so we learn from them?

You have those concepts at birth because you do not learn.

The trouble is that this sort of thing is often passed down and young children don't know any different.

Ye didna need to know because it's given to ye on a plate and ye eat it up and it gets inside ye God help us!

Rab then went on to talk about many other general matters relating to the spirit world including, for example, gardening, fairies, water, the halls of learning, food and drink and his own living arrangements. He was asked:

What other things do you do besides coming to speak to us?

Well, I like to do some readin' to make up for lost time. Make up for lost time when I was on the earth too busy fightin,' not enough time learnin,' reading,' gettin' the knowledge. So I'm making up some time now.

Do you go to the Halls of Learning?

Ah, I go to the Halls of Learnin' and I listen a lot to what folk have to say. Yes there's experience to be gained from listening to the experiences of others.

What type of things do they talk about in the Halls of Learning?

All manner of things. I don't mean the Halls of Learnin' alone. I mean just talking, passin' the time of day, though we don't have a day. Passin' the time of day with people. Reminiscin,' recantin' stories, experiences, good and bad, beautiful and not so beautiful, but all beautiful in their way because they are all learnin.'

Where did you find yourself when you passed over? Did you have loved ones come to meet you?

Aye, I had loved ones and I met some of those English. Met a few of those English lads, which I had put to rest. Not easy. Wasna easy.

Rab continued to describe the spirit world:

It's beautiful here. Beautiful!

Have you a nice place to live now?

Aye, I've got a nice place. I have a beautiful stone cottage.

Is it similar to the kind of building you had in your day?

Similar in a manner of speaking, but it's different also. But it's beautiful.

Do you live on your own?

I've got some of me family with me.

What is the water like in the spirit world?

The water constantly shimmers in the light. It's beautiful the way it reflects the light and the surroundins.' Beautiful. You talk about the water of life here (earth), but here, where I am, it is *really* like the water of life.

Have you seen fairies?

Aye, I've seen fairies. You may perhaps if you're looking too while you're here. (On earth) You reach out to them when you're back in your garden or in the wood in a quiet bit, a quiet space. You reach out to them with your love and who knows?

Do you have any other kind of work, apart from helping people come over?

I lead me band of brigands around causing mayhem, lassie. I'm only joking with ye, lassie. I travel around and meet them what come over. I do some growing flowers and plants.

Do you create those yourself or do you have to ask someone else to create them for you?

We do our bit but there's them that helps.

Are there always enough people who can and will help you do these things?

Oh, aye, there's many a willin' soul, many a willin' soul ready to help you. There's no standin' back, no pullin' back.

It sounds a lovely place to be in. Are there any disadvantages at all?

Rab laughs and responds:

Aye, there's no bloody English to fight.

Can you eat fruit?

Aye, we can eat fruit and we can drink the wine. We drink the wine out of the fruit.

Can you also drink tea if you want?

Aye, ye can drink all manner of things if you want. Why bother with tea when ye've got something else. Ye grow out of it. Ye get used to life here and ye grow out of it. There's plenty else to do, plenty of enjoyment to be had without needing drink or food.

It's difficult to imagine a life where you haven't got to cook or clean.

Ah, but it's true, lassie. You dina need to cook or clean or dig your garden or whatever else you're used to here. Dina need to do that.

But is there enough to do?

If ye wanna spade, lassie, we'll give ye one. We'll fix it so ye can dig your earth too if you want. I think ye'd get tired of that. Ah, I'm sure ye'd get tired of that. Have ye not done enough diggin' here already? Ye can do it all other ways.

What does it feel like talking through a medium?

It feels funny. It takes some getting used to as it does for the medium. But we both get used to it, and then it gets easier.

Can you tell if the right words are coming out?

Aye, most of the time. He has got to go with it; (Paul) go with the flow to help it along. We know it ain't easy.

Have you had a glimpse of your earlier lives yet?

Well, I've not been too worried about that. Got enough thinking about me last one. More than enough without delving back.

*   *   *

Billy

Billy also had killed someone when on the earth plane; however, his circumstances were a little different from Rab. Like so many other spirits, Billy's personality seemed pretty much as you would imagine him on earth. Nevertheless, as our conversation unfolded it became obvious that he had moved on somewhat from the views he held whilst in his last incarnation. Billy's communication is quite long; however, we decided to include it all; firstly, because he demonstrates so well the humour that we know exists in the spirit world but also, regardless of the humorous dialect running through our conversation he still manages to put across the more serious points that were obviously dear to his heart. He also makes a serious attempt to explain to us just what things like mountains and water are made of in the spirit world, also the meaning of "ethereal" sex.

Billy came through with a strong American accent and whilst it is impossible to exactly reconstruct in text the real flavour of the conversation, we have, nevertheless, attempted to record it as near as possible to the way it was communicated to us.

The communication started with some banter, with Billy pretending to be "Billy the Kid." He said:

No, I'm not really Billy the Kid but I'm Billy. If I impersonate Billy the Kid, he might come looking for me to put a hole into me.

So you come from America then?

I come from America yeah I sure do.

How long ago was that, Billy?

Well I don't rightly know. I guess if I was spitting into the wind to figure it out I'd reckon it would be something like two hundred years—something like that.

It was some time ago then?

Some time ago—may be nothing.

What did you do?

I was a bit of a gun fighter.

Were you hired by people?

No I was only a part-time gun fighter ha ha, when people riled me, you follow me.

You mean you shot people if you didn't (Billy interrupted)

I defended myself, mam. I defended myself.

Were you a cowboy?

I was no cowboy. I didn't fancy those smelly boots. Trailing behind a whole herd of cattle—it never did appeal to me, especially if you take up the rear trail. It gets mighty dirty, dusty, back there and the smell, if the wind's in the wrong direction, gets pretty powerful. No I would not recommend that, mam.

So what did you do to earn a living?

To earn a living? I did a bit of prospecting, I did a bit of shop keeping, I did a bit of riling people up. I did a bit of sitting on the duck boards, rocking me rocking chair. I did a bit of this and I did a bit of that—bit of the other. And I mean the "other" folks (sex) ha ha.

And whereabouts did you do all this?

Billy laughed and replied:

I generally found it was better to do the "other" sir in an upstairs room (laughter) much more comfortable. But I know some folks were liable to use other places but generally I did not find them so comfortable and you gotta have due regard to comfort of the lady, Yeah.

Billy, can you still have sex in the spirit world?

Well, folks, you sure can but not quite like what you have on your plane. But I guess it's a more rarefied form of sex. But beautiful for all that and indeed I would highly recommend it. It's inspiring, this ethereal sex. It's a more exaggerated form in some respects, folks, because it really does connect you to the other party—in a way you're not always connected to the other party even when you are connected to them, if you follow my drift.

Is this the "blending" we hear about?

Yes it sure is a blending.

So do you take your clothes off for this blending?

What clothes would we be talking about?

Well you can clothe yourself if you want to, can't you?

Well you can have imaginary clothes if you wish to have them. You could walk around the place stark naked as well of course though that may attract a few eyes but they would soon get bored with that. But yeah, you can connect and you do not need to seriously take off your clothes so to speak because your spiritual energies may connect without the inconvenience of taking off your clothes. You follow?

I'm only curious because I have just read a book on spirit communication, which talks a lot about sex in the spirit world.

Billy laughed and responded:

You can, of course, get up to all kinds of things if you leave your clothes on, without them folks not necessarily clocking what you're up to.

What kind of things are we talking about Billy?

Like blending. What other kinds of things have you got in mind?

Do you mean the other person doesn't know what you're up to?

No, I do not mean that, mam. I mean those parties what might be taking an interest in the vicinity are not necessarily aware, though I must admit they would have to be seriously blind to not spot it at all.

But yeah, you can blend; you can connect without taking no clothes off and without going to a secret place.

Billy suddenly went off on a different theme. He told us:

You know, when I was last on your plane we had these marshals and what have you, these sheriffs of these towns. I generally found that sometimes they could be obnoxious folk. You know it's like some guy said to himself, well, I'd really like to rule this roost. I would really like to throw my weight around. I would really like to be noticed by people, so I'll put this badge on to give me the excuse to do it. You follow me, folks? So I believe there is something in this that may be of interest to you folks in your time, for you sometimes get this happening in your day. I don't mean you get any gun-toting sheriffs around your place but I do mean that you sometimes get folks aspiring to and taking on positions of authority and power to throw their weight around. You understand me, folks? So you see these positions of authority and power, these roles that they take on are an excuse to vent their wishes, their desires, on the populous who happen to be unfortunate enough to get in the way. You understand me?

So we have this problem about people looking out for these roles, these posts that they may use to vent their desire, to express themselves in the way in which they'd like to express themselves. So in this we've got a problem of course, yeah. But then there are always these other folks who are willing to take on these jobs, these roles of responsibility and just do it for the good of their hearts, for the sake of the people; to help the people, to do something to help to make a difference. So that's obviously a better motivation than in the case of the other folks. So I'm sure you get this in your times.

Does it surprise you how America has changed in two hundred years?

Well not too much. I can still see plenty of folks toting guns around the place. Guns got a bit bigger with time and they seem to have a lot of communal guns in these times what they call missiles. Yeah, so they sort of get carried on in this way I guess, which started some time ago. It's fortunate in some respects, folks, 'cause folks in some societies, they get on a bit of a roller coaster and they can't get off—if you follow my drift. So they get into this sort of mind set, this sort of way of viewing things, this sort of way of conducting business and they get sort of stuck on the roller coaster, if you follow me—yeah instead of thinking, what the hell am I doing on this roller coaster and where the hell is it taking me. They just stay glued onto it and it gets them into all kinds of trouble. So it's a good thing once in a while, folks, to look at the roller coaster, the particular one you happen to be on at the time and think, well where is it really taking me and do I really want to be on this roller coaster or should I be jumping ship or looking for a new one to jump onto that would take me in a more positive direction.

There was a pause from Billy and someone decided to ask another question:
Did you kill anyone when you were last on the earth plane, Billy?

Billy didn't answer that question right away. He continued:

You know the strongest nation on your earth needs to be the most silent nation in some respects. I know they have responsibility because of their power but also they have responsibility to show—what you call it—show example yeah. No better way to show modesty, an example of modesty, of humility, when you got all the power in the world.

You agree with me, folks? Therefore, it's a pity my compatriots don't show a bit more of that; quietness, a reluctance to act, to get involved, unless they're asked to get involved. You understand me? Yeah too quick to get involved. I'm not saying that they shouldn't get involved, cause they should too, but they should be a bit more backward in coming forward yeah.

Billy decided to answer the previous question:

What did you say to me? Did I knock anyone off on my last visitation to earth? Well unfortunately, mam, I had to knock someone off because he had a determined eye to knock **me** off.
So it was self-defence?
Yeah it was self-defence and he didn't have a hope in hell of defence because he was a bit foolish, not to say stupid because there was no way he was going to beat me to the draw. But on the other hand if I didn't draw I'd have been one dead Billy, yeah.
So how does this affect you now?

This affects me in a mortifying way 'cause I know about sanctity of life now and much more so than I knew when I was on your earth last time. So it mortifies me to have to come to terms with the fact that I had to kill old Freddie. But you know old Fred was like a bear with a headache half the time, a bear with a headache with a trigger-happy finger. Not a good combination, sir. Not a good combination when you're stood facing that barrel so you gotta do your thing to protect yourself. So I'm sorry for old Fred but I had to do my bit. I had to do what I had to do at the time.

Was he the only one you killed?

Yeah he was the only one. I had a reputation. Some folks knew my reputation and were therefore having the good sense not to try out something on me, yeah.

So was your reputation for being fast then—not for killing people?

For being able to protect myself, and therefore folks did not push their luck too far. Some times, of course, you'd get them folks who felt they had to go and try it out. But I did not bite the bait. So, you see, although I was accomplished, you might say, in my art, I did not take the bait where I didn't need to take the bait. So I was what you would call in control. Lot more in control than poor old Fred with his headache.

Have you met Fred since being in the spirit world?

Yeah I met him since and I said to him, "Oh you stupid old Fred, what the hell did you go and shoot at me for like that. You knew damn well I'd get you first." Yeah but, he say, "Well yea never can tell, you just don't know your luck on the day." But I said, "Well sure as hell, Fred your luck wasn't with you that day."

So he doesn't hold any grudge?

No he don't hold no grudges, so we shared a pint of ale since we come over.

How did you make your transition to the spirit world, Billy?

Speedily.

You weren't shot?

No I was not shot. I recall I had a fall, which bashed my head and before I knew what had happened I was in the arms of my favourite lover, yeah. But there was something different, something strange going on. When I looked around things weren't right. They weren't looking like they should have been looking, so I knew then there was something going on. Yeah, so I said to old Dolly. "What the hells going on here Dolly? This don't look right." And she explained everything to me, yeah and that's fine.

So had she already passed on?

Yeah, she'd passed on.

There followed some hilarious discussion about who might have been holding him (if anyone) on the *earth plane* when he died. Billy certainly couldn't cope with the thought that his hairy old friend had held him in his arms as he lay dying. His banter was as fast as any comedian we've heard and was certainly as funny. Billy makes further reference to this later on. The questions continued:

So, Billy, did you need to go into one of the hospitals in the spirit world?

No I didn't need no hospital. No. I just stayed in the comfort of my favourite lover's arms, which was very pleasant once I got used to the surroundings, which were so different.

Where were you when you woke up?

I was in the countryside, but countryside the like of which I'd never seen before. It was so sort of—I don't know how to describe it to you—it was sort of there and not there. It was sort of hard rock but not hard rock. It was—it was like it was energy. It was like—I'll see if I can think of something for you poor folk who haven't witnessed this yet—not lately any rate—. If I can think of some way to describe this to you. It's not easy though—. It was like as if the mountains were made out of water but I'm not saying that they looked like water, I'm saying that they looked like mountains. Do you follow me? They looked like mountains but it was as if they had the "flavour" of water. I don't know if that helps you folks?

Is that because you felt that they were moving?

It's like they were alive. I think that's the best I can do for you—to compare it to like as if they were made of water, sheet of water—for water that had all the texture and the colour of real mountains. You follow? And it was like that with everything else too. It was like everything was alive. Of course I know trees are alive in your plane but it was like these trees were especially alive and their life had something in common with the life of the mountains—and the life of the water on this land of ours too.

And did it feel real, Billy?

Oh yeah it felt real, mam. It felt mighty real. More real I'd say than your place. More real than your place 'cause as I say, this substance whatever it is, whatever you call it, I'd say to you it's within everything you can see too. But it's as if it's the spiritual essence of what you see before you—beautiful, mam, beautiful.

Do you remember going through a dark tunnel when you died?

I don't rightly remember that but it all happened so fast I suspect I could have been through any number of tunnels and not been aware of them, it was all happening so fast, mighty fast, yeah—yeah faster than that bullet that went through poor old Fred's head.

There was some further chitchat and laughter, about the way Billy had died, and then he was asked:

What kind of things do you do now in the spirit world?

Well I get around. I like the nature, the natural world of this place. I do some work along those lines with the natural world of this place— the animal and the birds, the bees, the fishes. I spend a lot of time in communion with those animals. And it's beautiful because you can commune with these creatures where you could not commune with them, or at least not like you can here when you're on the earth plane. It's a beautiful experience, folks, passing the time of day with a trout.

One member of our group, who is particularly interested in Native American people, asked:

Did you know any American Indians when you were on the earth plane, Billy?

Well, there weren't too many American Indians; at least not in the part of America that I lived in, because generally they had moved them to some other part of America, if you follow my drift. I'm not saying I'm pleased about that, especially since I came up here because I know that there should have been different rules applied but that's the way it was in those days, yeah, and those Indians weren't—what you call it?—they weren't no soft pussies. Some were a pretty mean bunch of people. But they, like all the other folks, were a mixed bunch of critters.

I came across a real wise one once—real wise Indian. He knew the way of life, knew the way of living, that's for sure.

What was his name?

Well he was a Blackfoot Indian. Can't rightly remember his name though. May come to me if you talk a bit more.

Where you in the area of America where the Blackfoots were?

Yeah, I was generally in that part but, like I say, they moved them off a bit but generally around that area yeah. I'm still trying to remember the Blackfoot Indian's name for this gentleman (referring to the person asking the question) but you see I could not remember his name when on the earth plane once I'd left him so what hope have you got to get this name from me now (laughing) but I can probably find out. I could probably go and ask old Fred or someone to help me, so long as he didn't tell me about my death.

Billy was back again to his speculation of who might have held him when he was dying, which again created much laughter. What he said next is an interesting concept. Billy told us:

Got to be careful, because I've had that thought now. Now that thought would have got broadcast you know and sent out. I could have any number of tricksters coming up to me now and telling me all kinds of things. I wouldn't be at all surprised if I found myself being found dead in the arms of fifty people or more.

So they will all know now, will they?

Oh yeah, you gotta watch your thoughts on this side. I'm only hoping that because I'm talking to you folks, the thought goes through a sort of filter; well not filter but it goes through a sort of mist. I'm hoping that it will get sort of diffused a bit before it hits too many on this side. Apart from if they're listening to me directly from here of course, which I've got a real problem with. I hadn't bargained for this when I came here tonight. You got me in all kinds of trouble now with this train of thought. I think I'm gonna have to put this name business to one side for a minute. (Billy was still trying to remember the name of the Black Foot Indian) It may come back to me. If I come back to you sometime maybe I can tell you then.

It was time to finish.

I'm afraid it's time to finish now, Billy.

Yeah, I know it's time for me to hit the trail. I'm mighty glad that our paths have crossed on the trail though, folks. I'm glad. I've enjoyed my time, my conversation with yea. Hope you didn't find my manner too bruising. I know you get some high faluting folk through, these philosophy folk to talk to you.

As a *final* remark, Eileen commented that we'd had a pirate and a conquistador communicate in the past. Billy was off again:

Yeah, well, I think there's some merit in all these interesting folk coming through to you. I think you'd soon get bored with all these high and mighty philosophical guys and I think we all got something to offer in our own different ways. So I'll leave yer, my friends. I'll leave yer now, hit the trail and hop on my horse. Ride off into the horizon like on those films you see. Except the horizon I'm riding off into is all light. I'm not riding off into any night sky, setting sun. No I'm riding off into the bright light of the spirit lands, to which I would seriously commend you.

Billy "final" comments brought forth another question from a member of our group so Billy continued, this time on a different theme, for a few minutes more. What he had to say was again of particular interest. He was asked:

Do you miss the setting sun, Billy?

Well we can have the setting sun if we want it. We can create things, we can ask for them to order, you see, if you want them. So we don't miss out on nothing. Could miss out on some of the real physical-type things sometimes but you know there's so much to make up for that; you don't miss them and if you really desperately miss them you can always come back, if you're foolish enough, can't yer. I know there is a time for coming back though sometimes, so I wouldn't berate it.

Can you visit parts of the earth if you choose to?

Yeah, you can, you sure can, Arnie. You can visit any place you want if you want to, yeah.

In any time?

Well that's a bit different.

Could you go back to your own childhood?

Not any time, in your sense of coming back here but you could visit in the sense of connecting with it through the—well the best I can do for you is to say connecting to it through the Internet (laughter.) That sort of portrays, or gives a picture for what I want to convey to you. It's not quite like that of course, but a good comparison yeah. You with me? But it's more like an inter-dimensional Internet, if it's an Internet and it's more like—you know I said this substance, everything, is made out of this sort of watery stuff. Well it's like as if you can imagine all this watery stuff and all these mountains, lands and all, all coming out from a sort of almighty whirlpool. A whirlpool with a quiet centre yeah. But on all the outside you got all this creation stuff going on and all these whorls. It's like I said if you dip your finger in the centre of that whirlpool, that watery stuff, the essence of that watery stuff you can connect with your time gone by. You with me, Arnie?

Yes sort of.

Well, sort of, is the best you're going to do I'm afraid, 'cause it ain't easy to portray it.

Someone else asked:

So is that different to coming back here in the present day, like now?

Yeah 'cause it's like you're able to connect with your own time that you've lived through that's gone by. You can do that for other times too of course, but Arnie asked me about connecting with a time that you've been through. So you can do it that way and it's like you're almost there, because you connect with it. But it's not like coming back to this world of yours now and experiencing things in this way you understand (medium thumped his chest) but nearest damn to it. In some ways it's as real, for it's truly the essence of that moment you live through that you connect with.

Do you have to go to the Halls of Learning to do that?

Well, no, you don't have to. You can do it there, but you can do it in some other places also yeah.

Do you need training to do it?

Well I wouldn't go dipping your finger in that whirlpool without some serious advice, ha ha. You could get yourself in some unpredictable situations.

We'd overrun and it really was time for Billy to go. Billy recognised this and said his farewell:

Well I'm going to finally get on the horse and hit the trail that I was going to do all those minutes ago. And I'm going to doff my hat to you folks in farewell and I wish you all the best. I pray sincerely that your guns can stay in your holsters. So, bye to you folks. Bye, my friends—my new friends—bye.

*   *   *

Black Beard

Black Beard came at the end of a very quiet night when we'd been sitting for physical phenomena. The conversation started with him giving us some advice and assurance about our activities. He talked about his life and the fact that he'd killed for monetary gain. It is interesting to note both the differences and the similarities between Black Beard and Rab in their attitude towards killing and how that affected their conditions in the spirit world.

Black Beard initially presented as very much like a pirate who seemed unrepentant about his life on earth, although he was keen to tell us that he was not the Black Beard that was recorded in our history books. Later, his more serious side became apparent. A member of the group asked:

Do you know what the spirit group have been doing tonight with the energies?
No they've been scouting around trying to pull a bit of energy out of you lot.
We have certainly all been yawning, but we haven't noticed any difference in the atmosphere tonight.
Well you never know. It's a funny thing, you know, sometimes you can be doing nothing it would seem and sometimes it can simply happen—just like that. It's all or nothing with it, you see—all or nothing with it.
What kind of things do you do in the spirit world?

Sail the seas and a goodly occupation it be too. And a less difficult operation it be too than when I was on your seas. Your seas are rough and tough.

Were you a sailor when on earth?

Aye I was that. I was a sailor of the seven seas, aye with me scull and crossbones at the top of the mast, ha.

Were you a pirate then?

Aye, lad.

So you sail currently?

Ha, you gotta sail currently, lad. You gotta make the best use of the currents.(laughter)

Do you still have your old crew with you?

Aye I got some of them. Some of them became landlubbers.

Did you get your boat as soon as you went over to the spirit world or did you have to wait for it?

Got the boat on condition, ha. You can guess the condition.

That you mended your ways?

Yes.

And have you?

Well I've still got my boat, haven't I?

What was your job on the boat?

I was the captain, aye. I spotted the game with me telescope.

Did you have to go to those people after and say you were sorry?

Black Beard laughed and replied:

Oh aye, I went to them and said I am very sorry ha ha ha for relieving you of your treasure that wasn't your treasure. (more laughter)

But it wasn't your treasure either, was it?

Well that's a matter of opinion.

What did you do with the treasure when you got it?

Kept it. (With much laughter) I wasn't running some benevolent society.

Did you make your self a very rich man then?

Aye I was rich, lass, aye. I was rich and me crew were rich too. I took from the rich and gave to the poor. Ha, gave to the poor, me crew.

Did it benefit you? Did you feel any happier?

It benefited me greatly. It made me feel very happy to see that gold coin in me coffers. Made me crew happy to see the gold coin too. Aye passing the gold coin for a tankard of ale.

Did you ever have a mutiny on your boat?

No my crew were a happy crew, no sweat for them sailing the seven seas.

Do you still have the seven seas in the spirit world?

Aye and the rest.

What were you before you were a pirate?

I served me time in Her Majesty's navy briefly. I learned the ropes, ha, and by God you needed to learn the ropes to stay alive.

What made you turn to piracy when you had a job in the navy?

When you been in Her Majesty's navy there was many a good reason to turn to piracy—to get your own back for one.

Black Beard started to reminisce about his life on earth. He continued:

Beautiful sea in the full sailing rig filled by the wind—aye beautiful cutting through the waves, dancing through the white waves—aye beautiful.

What did you learn from your life?

I learnt to out-manoeuvre the enemy. I learnt to fill me coffers. I learnt to keep me crew happy. I learnt to outwit that would outwit me. But I don't think you're asking me about that. I should hope not anyway.

Black Beard became more serious:

Did you have a pseudonym when you were a pirate? Did you get a reputation?

Aye, I got a nasty reputation but then that's warped—good reputation with me crew.

Well, I don't suppose you could have been a nice pirate, could you?

Oh I was a benevolent pirate with me crew—beautiful crew.

If you had your life again, would you choose the same kind of life?

Black Beard Smiled and replied:

No I cannot say I would, lass. You've been fishing for this I know. Oh you are boring people. No I would not. I would like to live in the sea again. I love the sea, the elements of the sea and the wind in your hair and the sails. I love the sea. Aye it's beautiful. You know, you go off into the ocean and you can't see land. Can't see land no matter where you look and yet it's such a sweet sight when you see it again, lass—such a sweet sight. It's worth being away for months on end to see it again. Makes you appreciate it; beautiful sight. You can smell the sweet smell of the land you know when you're coming back from miles away. You can smell it. You've got a good nose for it and by God you get a good nose for it after you've been away some time. You smell it from miles away. It's a sweet smell, beautiful smell and when you see them birds—you get watching for them birds and then you know you're near land—beautiful experience yes.

How did you manage to dock? Everyone must have known you were a pirate.

I owned the docks, lass (laughs.) I owned the whole damn island. No one meddled with me. But you're right, I wouldn't do it again—dabbled a bit too much with people's lives and what have yer, yes. It's not nice, is it? No it's not nice—no.

Did you ever meet up with other pirates?

Oh yes we met sometimes. Sharing stories, exaggerating our exploits, bit like fishermen exaggerating the catch they get. Had some good times but, you know, it's not nice to go cutting people's throats. on account they can't talk to yer then, ha, and share experiences with yer. Can't get any sense out of them when you ask them questions. No, I've learnt it's more joyful to talk to folks than slit their throats. Interesting some folks, when you listen to them rather than slitting their throats—aye.

So do you listen to others' experiences now?

Oh aye we put into port here and we put into port there and we show people over our boat and we talk to folk and we have a drop of ale.

And is your boat a replica of the boat you had on earth?

Ah it is, lad.

So people can see it was a pirate boat?

Oh yes, oh yes. I don't have the scull and cross bones at the top of the mast no more. It wouldn't go down well, you see, bit squeamish some folk. Might give them a bad impression, the wrong impression that we have slipped in from the nether regions.

Talking about the nether regions, Black Beard, did you have to go there when you passed over?

Not exactly—not exactly. Had to do some learnin' before I got to where I am now though. But not exactly—I was an honest cutthroat. Ha ha.

We've heard of this before. Rab said it made a difference what your attitude to killing was.

I had no malice in me, but I had to do some learnin' all the same, aye. It was all a big game to me you see, lass. But no game when people are loosing their lives is it? So we had to mend our ways.

What was the name for your boat?

Bloody Mary (adds very quickly) but I don't call it that no more now.

After we'd all finished laughing Black Beard continued:

Well I think I need to catch the tides and the winds.

Eileen asked if he had been to the South of France. Black Beard responded:

No I ain't been near your south of France. I've been sailing the turquoise seas, crossing between the islands. Some folks like to live on islands, you know, like they like them over there, where you are. I like the islands because there's lots of sea in between them, ha. Well I must go. If you want me to come through again you just holler to the man with the paddle and ask for Back Beard—not the one *you* know of, mind.

Is there a famous Black Beard?

Infamous: I was kinder hearted than him.

Were you before or after him?

About the same time—black beard and red heart. I'll better go. I hope it's not been too gory for yer, but I have mended me ways, aye I've mended me ways.

It's good to hear as well that you didn't end up in the depths of the darker regions.

No not the depths—the shallows.

You just paddled, did you?

I floated on me raft. So I'll be going and wishing for fair winds for yer, all my friends and plenty of currents to go with yer. Farewell to yer.

Chapter 8

Liberace

One famous spirit who has visited us on a number of occasions is Liberace (a famous pianist whom died some years ago.) We discovered later that Davia had sought him out because of Eileen's affection for him and love of his music. His first attempt to come through was blocked by my sceptical mind, which I referred to earlier. However, he proved persistent.

This particular night we were sitting alone. When Eileen had gotten over the shock of finding herself speaking to her favourite pianist, the conversation flowed like that of two friends talking together. Following the initial social chitchat, Liberace or Lee, as he is known, talked about some of the emotional pain he'd endured in the last days of his life. Eileen asked:

Have you managed to adjust to the spirit world after the glamour of your earth life?

Yeah. It's not been too easy at times being here, because when you've lived the kind of life I've lived on earth it takes a bit of getting used to.

Can you still play the piano?

Yeah, I can play the piano.

It was through listening to your records that I developed a love of classical music.

Yeah, I know that. I'm glad of that.

I came to see you at the Palladium.

Yeah, it's a beautiful theatre that. We had it all kitted out.

Yes the water fountain was lovely.

It was quite something, wasn't it?

And your costumes!
You liked my costumes?
Yes, I did.
Which one did you like the best?
I think the one with the white fur.
You liked all my jewels?
Yes and your rings.

I didn't used to dress like that, you know. I learnt that you need to make a splash. And people liked that. They enjoyed that and I enjoyed it too. It worked for both of us, a bit of enjoyment.

And your dancing.

You liked my dancing? I practised hard at that, you know. It's not natural but I developed a talent.

We sometimes play your CD at our sittings, Lee.

Yeah, I've been listening to it. I wish I could join along.

Are you with your mother in the spirit world?

Yeah, I'm with, mom. Yes, we enjoy it here. Those last days were hard, yes, but we enjoy it here.

It was a shame the way things turned out.

It hurts here (touching his heart area) it hurts.

Yes, but you gave a lot to people when you were on earth, a lot of pleasure, a lot of enjoyment.

Yeah, it felt like they were trying to rubbish all that though, in them final days.

That's the way people are unfortunately and they were very early days of AIDS too. People don't make such a fuss about it now; at least not in this country. You were unfortunate being born at the time you were; for the type of life that you had; and what you had to go through with prejudice.

Yeah, old poor Rocky (Rock Hudson) had a hard time too. You play my song sometimes and I'll play along in spirit.

Good, I'll do that.

It's nice, you know, because we can share that moment in some ways. You play your music down here and I can play along in spirit. So we share the moment.

Lee, have you made many friends in the spirit world?

I've made some friends and I've met a lot of others, old friends. (Lee deviated) My hands are bigger than his.) (Referring to Paul)

So Paul can feel the difference, can he?

OK for playing the piano though.

Are you able to still have your concerts in the spirit world?

Yes and it gives me great joy, great joy. Yes it helps, it helps a lot, to give people joy. There were things I had to learn.

Do you still dress up for concerts?

Yes, for old times sake.

I read your book.

What did you make of it?

I thought it was excellent. Did you give away all your belongings when you were very ill?

Yes, I gave them away and started again. I thought it was over so I decided to give things away to make a clean sweep.

And then you made all your money again.

Yes.

You must have had a talent for making money, Lee.

A talent for doing a good show.

Are you doing any particular work in the spirit world?

I'm doing my concerts and I have to spend some time learning, reflecting on my life. I've got some reflecting to do still. Yes. Some things were not too good. I had to rethink some of my ideas.

I suppose we will all have to do that.

Yeah, but some of us have bigger ones to rethink than others. You know when you are in the spotlight, when you live the kind of life that I lived in the spotlight, you can get distracted and distorted—it can go down tracks it's best not gone down. So you gotta rethink. But there are understanding folks up here, understanding folks. They help you.

Rab, when he came through to talk to us, described how the guides "got him."

Yeah, I believe so. They can be some tough cookies. They don't take "no" for an answer and they don't go away when you tell them to.

I suppose it must be difficult for anyone who is in the limelight. I expect many people are forced into doing things they wouldn't normally do because of the demands and pressures.

Yeah, well there are demands made on all of us, aren't there? And I guess I succumbed to some of those demands myself.

Have you heard anything of Diana since she passed over? (the Princess of Wales)

We know of her. She had a good heart. She had troubles, but she had a good heart. It's sad to die so young.
Is Rock Hudson settled now?
Yeah.

        *   *   *

On another occasion Liberace (Lee) immediately followed a singer called Georgina. She began her communication by singing to us and her following banter was light-hearted. She was asked if she'd met our friend Liberace in the spirit world. Georgina replied laughingly.

Ah yes we know of old Lee. He was an excellent piano player and he still is and we have done a turn with him but the trouble is there is a bit of completion between us. Well, he liked the limelight and I like the limelight so we have a bit of a problem there. So we have to carve it up and share it out.

Almost immediately after this she disappeared and Lee came through. He seemed lighter-hearted on this occasion. All the members of our Home Circle were present and Lee told us about his music and other things in the spirit world. He began:

Yeah, it's me. She was going on something (going on too long) so I thought I'd better come through to share our limelight. I know it's been some time. Not very long, of course, for us but I know it's been some time for you.

Introductions took place. Then Lee asked:
You listen to my music. What did you think of it?
It was very entertaining and happy as well.
Good, this was important to me. I would play around a bit with music, as you know to get it right for people, to make it enjoyable for them.
We were saying recently that your music always had that little bit extra that we could always recognise, Lee.
I try to give it my own imprint and style.
I like the "Boogie Woogie."

You like that one? I did, it was my favourite yeah. Liked that "Jack the Knife" too.

I liked the glittery suits and the flamboyance as well.

I had a lot of them, didn't I? You should have seen my wardrobes. I needed nearly as many wardrobes as I needed suits.

Lee, were all your suits kept after you died?

I understand a lot of them were yeah.

Do you have the equivalent in the spirit world or do you have something completely different now?

I can wear something completely different every day—no cleaning problems. I could wear something completely different every minute of every day if I want to.

Do you compose any music yourself?

Well I've tried my hand at that and had some success but I still like to perform; it's my first love to perform.

Even in the spirit world?

Oh yeah, especially so in the spirit world. Music is very important to us here, you know. It is important on the earth plane also of course but it is no less important, if anything *more* important in the spirit world. The whole place seems to vibrate with music and melody. You cannot look at anything without sensing a melody in it with the harmony sounding throughout the whole place. The sights and sounds all mingle—beautiful place but I know your friends (our spirit group) here have told you of this many a time. They promised you a tour.

Lee, with you being musical, are you especially attuned to that side of the spirit world or is everybody attuned in the same way?

You gotta be attuned here to do much good (laughs) yes. We are attuned to the musical side. We are attuned to the harmony of sound but it's there for all to see, for all to hear, a beautiful thing, a gift of life.

Have you had to learn new instruments in the spirit world that relate to a piano?

You mean do I play in concert with other instruments?

Well I didn't know whether they would have a piano in the spirit world.

They have the equivalent of a piano, which sounds just like a piano but it's got a special quality to it here and we can play with others, orchestras, instruments in the auditorium—more like an amphitheatre, yeah.

Do you still do a bit of a dance?

Oh you saw that (laughter) that was hard work for me.

I remember your words, "I've got guts."

Well I practised that hard. I practised that for many an hour, I guess. Overall it was hard work but I enjoyed doing that. It used my energy up though, needed to sit down at the piano again after.

You know that Davia (our comedian stage manager) has been practising your smile. *

*For a while following Lee's first visit, Davia, to everyone's amusement, would make a very good job of mimicking Lee's smile.

Lee replied:

I heard of that. He's got a mighty posse on his trail. No one is safe from him, no. But he is a generous soul. He is a warm soul.

Some light-hearted discussion followed about Davia, and then Lee commented:

But, you know, you will find it hard to outwit us, because there is an awful intelligence service here. You ain't seen networking like this. He's watching and listening, you know.

It was time to finish. It was Christmas times and Lee finished off the communication with his best wishes.

*   *   *

Well I think my time has come up so I think I'll have to leave you. But I'm pleased to have made your acquaintance and once we've made an acquaintance there's a link. So I would hope that we can talk again sometime. Until we meet again I would give you my smile, (laughs) but I know you are at a disadvantage. (The session was held in a dark room.)

I thank you and I would wish you a happy Christmas and a joyous New Year. Perhaps we have a duo again sometime.

Chapter 9

Charles Dickens

The range of spirit visitors has been quite remarkable. Sometimes we've been told that this has been encouraged in order to develop and refine Paul's ability to function as a medium for the communication. The range of spirits, it seems, offers good practise opportunities and stretches his abilities. The relationship link, which might prompt a visit from many of our visitors, is often tenuous if not totally non-existent, though even an interest in the period in which they lived can seem to provoke a visit from someone. However, there is usually a deeper purpose to the visit, which often only becomes apparent as the communication progresses and often in a disarming way.

The following visitor came just as we were preparing the second edition of this book for publication. A few nights prior to his visit we'd been watching a TV programme about a trip he took to Canada and the US. Charles explained how this link had helped the communication to take place. Also our daughter, Emma, has a cherished life ambition to be a writer. She does not often get the opportunity to attend our meetings but on this particular occasion she had made a special effort to be present. She was not disappointed.

Charles began the conversation with:

You are quite learned; yes I think you are all quite learned, studied.

Someone in the group responded:
And are you quite learned?
I was a man of "letters" when I was last in your realm. I was a writer.

Have you talked to us before?
No I have not talked to you before but I have visited other groups before.
What type of books did you write?
I used to write "Dickensian" books.
You mean Dickens's time?
Yes.
Did you know Dickens?
Well yes. Writing "Dickensian" books it was an advantage to know him.
So did you copy his work?
No, no it was original.

The penny dropped:
Are you Charles Dickens?
Laughs loudly and replies:
Yes.

After we'd all recovered from the shock of speaking to Charles Dickens, Eileen commented:

We watched a programme about you a few nights ago. You had a trip around America and Canada didn't you?
Yes, I thought I would take the opportunity to talk to you because by watching the programme, you formed a link with me, and so made it easier for me to come through to talk to you. This is how it works you see. If you link with us it facilitates the link; therefore, we are more able to link with you; this is the law of reciprocity.

Eileen asked Charles whether he'd visited British Columbia when in Canada. He replied:

I am not familiar with it and I did not miss it. It was too far but there were many places that I did visit and I am glad to have seen them all because it added to the interest of life. It gave me many things to think about, many experiences to mull upon. You know how you sometimes visit places which are strange, unusual, out of the ordinary and they are different to your every day experiences of life and you have the experience but then you find upon your return to your homeland that you have many memories of your travels, many images in your mind which you can then revisit and refine and to mull upon to form a proper view of them and your experiences. Therefore, a journey of some weeks may indeed become a journey of a lifetime for you are enriched and you have a wealth, a treasure chest within you that you can revisit at your liberty to reflect upon.

Did it help you to write?

It did indeed help me to write. The experiences that you have my dear lady are of the utmost importance when it comes to the art of the writer. For every experience you have can be revisited and expounded upon and penned in a thousand different guises. Therefore, every experience which you have (turns to Emma and smiles) my miss, you must think of it with versatility. And you must realise that while some people would pen it in one format and in one context, it is perfectly possible to pen it in dozens of formats and contexts; therefore, each experience can be used to the full in many different guises. This is part of the skill of the writer, to use such experiences with flexibility and enrich them as you do so.

Another member of the group asked:

Are you still writing now, in the spirit world?

I am my sir, I love words you see, and I still use them to convey thoughts and ideas and images.

Did you write some of your books such as Scrooge and Oliver Twist as a social statement?

Yes I did because I felt that a social statement was needed at times to reflect the concerns which I had of the day because there were many social evils in my time; some of them existed, were not perpetrated as such, but nevertheless existed and caused unspeakable trouble and discomfort to those who had to endure them; some evils were more actively perpetrated like the evil of slavery had been.

Some of your books seemed quiet dark.

Er dark, dark but with the intention of revealing the light.

What was your favourite book?

They were all my children so it is like asking one who is their favourite child; it is not appropriate.

Was it hard to get things published?

It was at times difficult but once you became known as a writer it became easier because it is like it gathered a momentum. And once momentum is gathered it becomes unstoppable so it became much, much, easier.

I thought society of that time would not always be happy with your books especially if they were criticising society.

Society is not prone to like being criticised especially those rulers of society who think they know best yet they have need of critics, those who would point out the flaws else the flaws will go unnoticed, bypassed, nothing will be done about them. Is this not so? For it is important for someone to point out the flaws and to engage people, the common people if you wish, in such reflection for it is the common people who have the power at the end of the day. And if you can only kindle the consciousness of the common people, the ordinary people, behind an idea then you have an unstoppable force.

What do you write about now?

I still write about human nature; it was my common theme and my primary purpose.

If you hadn't succeeded with your writing what do think you may have done with your life?

Charles laughs and replies:
Perhaps I would have been a clock maker.

Note: This was said with humour and was a reference to Jacob, another spirit visitor who was a clock maker when last on the earth plane. Jacob is featured in our second book "Unfolding The Lotus."

Charles continued:
There is a similarity in some ways for there is, in writing, a need for perfect timing and order underlying what many see to be a lack of order at times, but there is a need for underlying order; timing is essential.

So Jacob may have made a good author?

He would indeed have made a good author if he could only have applied himself. He had you know a lot of interesting experiences because his occupation brought him into contact with many different levels of society and many different personages. And therefore, they brought to his attention all the foibles of human nature and all its levels of affluence and frailty. So he had a rich source of material had he been predisposed to taking up the pen.

Charles then turned to Emma, our daughter and youngest member of the group. He told her:

But I have come for you, my child, so you must ask me any questions you wish while I am here.
Oh thank you but I'm just "gobsmacked" that you are here.
It is no use being "gobsmacked" because it hinders the vocal chords and in hindering the vocal chords we find that your questions dry up and you need your questions.

Emma responded:
I find it hard to set times for my writing. How did you manage?
You absorb yourself in it. You absorb yourself in it so that it does not become a matter of *time*—because when you are absorbed *time* is timeless; it's without significance. So you are absorbed in your love and time is of no consequence. You follow me? So you must find something in which you can become absorbed in, to the point where you are not watching the clock. And you will not want to watch the clock because you will be absorbed.
Did you ever consider writing poetry?
I did try to write some poetry but it was not my greatest effort. I felt prose was my greatest achievement though I did try my hand at poetry sometimes.
Did your work become famous while you were still on the earth plane?
Yes it had some familiarity with people while I was still on the earth plane and I can say that they did take up some of my thoughts. They thought about them, which is all I wanted; to cause thought, thinking.
Where were you educated?
I was educated in the south of your country. I was fortunate to be educated quite well but I would say that the greatest education began when I took charge of this mission myself. For there is no education which can compare with the education which you yourself put yourself through when you have decided the correct syllabus, rather

than the syllabus of some other person who has decided for you. It is far better to decide your own syllabus and pursue it with energy.

Someone else asked:

Is Emma better writing about social issues, then?

I do not say necessarily social issues but I say human issues, to decipher the human spirit, human nature, and human problems. This I think is the proper occupation of the writer, to enlighten the human condition, human dilemmas, human problems, problems of the spirit, yes; rather than to advocate.

Are you talking about writing about the spirit world or writing about things you see happening on earth?

I can embrace both aspects. I had an enriched life upon your earth plane where I was privileged to observe much of the human condition and many personages who, shall we say, had experiences, which they found somewhat difficult. However, I can also reflect upon the experiences of those in the spirit form who have had to wrestle with some of their experiences from the earthly plane in order to advance their understanding and development. Therefore, there is no dichotomy here. It is a continuation, an unfolding enlightenment of the human spirit both on the earth plane and on the spirit plane.

It's going to be a very big book then?

Well you do not have to cover it all in one book. It is better to focus upon one aspect at a time.

Did you know you were going to be a writer when you came to the earth plane?

Yes I knew.

Did you ever see a ghost?

I did once; a fleeting image, which leaves you wondering if, you've seen it or not. But I am of the opinion that I did.

Have you visited other groups and spoken through trance before?

Sometimes I have, yes. I visited a séance in London when on the earth plane. A lady friend interested me in it for a short time.

Did your characters actually exist?

It was mixture of things sometimes. Characters were strongly drawn upon from those whom I had observed or knew, to an extent. But I was quite capable of combining elements of their character with elements of a fictional nature. You have to be flexible and it is best to be flexible lest you be accused of drawing too strongly from life, which may incur libel (laughter.)

What were your impressions of America? The television programme suggested that you were disappointed with it.

America was an unusual country, vibrant in many ways, very vibrant but, yes, disappointing in some respects as regards the quality of society they had managed to manifest. The quality was an admirable sentiment but less readily observed in the reality of the day.

Have you a wish to come back to the earth plane?

Wish to come back? Well there is a thought I could write a book on. And in writing the book (laughs) it would keep me in the spirit land.

If you did come back would you be a writer again?

Yes I might well do that but whether I would be a famous writer is another matter, but I think I would be entrapped to yet write again.

Were you friendly with any other writers and which ones did you like?

I was friendly with many, yes. I like the work of Shelly. Yes I liked the work of Shelly because I felt he had the gift of poetry, which I aspired to.

Did you like Wordsworth?

Yes, but not to the same extent as Shelly. Wordsworth I felt was too,—rustic is the word closest to what I look for. His work had a certain something, but not something, if you know what I mean.

Did you come from a family of writers?

No I did not. My father, I think, tried to have a go of a kind but was not a writer as such. No I was in the main a solitary writer.

On average, how long did it take you to write a book?

Averages, there are no averages. Some took a lot longer than others as an average (laughs)

Did you have your own writing room at home?

I used to try to be disciplined and I would certainly write at a desk on a regular basis to help me to focus myself.

Did you know the kind of things you would write about before you came to the earth and did you have a purpose for writing?

Not to that extent but as I said I was occupied by the human condition and spirit and therefore my efforts revolved around this. You need a focal point, you see, for your writing. You need a mission, but not a mission in the sense of being a missionary, but in a sense of focus, of purpose. But this in turn must also be flexible else each work would become a repetition of the former. So it is rather a matter of giving your work focus but this focus can express itself in many varied ways. I recommend this attitude to you.

So your life was in many ways a contrast to many other people.

It was gifted, it was affluent by the standards of many and privileged by the standards of many, and I was fortunate to have such an easy life compared to many, yes.

What made you feel compassionate then?

You had only to look about you, my friend, to see the condition of so many people and having the contrast of my own circumstances compared to theirs, only an unfeeling soul would not be aware of the difference and not feel compassion.

Which authors do you like on the earth plane now?

I am not familiar with them as such but I have sympathy for those who try to illumine the topics of your day. But not just the topics of your day but in the context again of the human condition for the human condition is a continuity upon your earth, the expression which it must manifest through, the trials and tribulations which it must manifest through. And the social issues which you must tackle in each generation shift and vary but the human nature underlying all these things, in this there is continuity, and therefore, it is this continuity, which greatly exercises my mind. And I do believe this is the proper subject for the writer, the novelist, or the "documentarian."

Is that the message you came through to give us, about human nature?

It is an underlying reality of life, I do believe; therefore, it is something that unites us from one generation to the next. Even those generations, which have long gone, they have continuity, an identity with the human nature, which you express in your life today. Therefore, there is a continuity across time and a brotherhood, if you wish, across time, for we all manifest this human nature and we all struggle to manifest its highest qualities in adversity. Therefore, this is our common bond, our common uniqueness.

When famous people return to the spirit world do they sometimes channel their talents through people on the earth plane?

There are those who try to influence by projecting thoughts or influence. There are those who try to manifest some of their continuing thoughts through the good offices of those they can influence. If this is what you mean then yes it is true.

So could you do that to someone on the earth plane?

Well you could try to influence them, their thoughts, their thinking, and their ideas but then it is up to them. They have power; they are the captains of their ship. But we try, in the background, to influence as best we can, for the good.

So if Emma wanted to connect with you...

She has only to reach out. We will try to inspire as best we can but it will be her effort. She must put the best foot forward still. You must trust in your intuition and your inspiration—and let your inspiration flow. Do not constrict it, let it flow.

Now I must be on my way. The bell does toll. I shall be off. I may have the opportunity to visit you again at some point perhaps. If the opportunity is forthcoming I shall take it up. Goodbye then; Merry Christmas from little Tim.

Chapter 10

Fred

The following is another example of how a spirit will "drop in" simply to enjoy a chat. One night Eileen's Uncle Fred came through. Much of the communication was personal to Eileen, but we've provided the following short extract as it conveys the continuity and naturalness of the relationship between the earth and spirit planes. We'd recently had a family wedding and he told us:

"We can still attend your celebrations from our side just as though we were still on the earth plane."

Fred was asked:

Did you have to go to a resting place when you passed, to recover?

Just for a little time. It wasn't too much trouble though, adjusting. When you meet other people you soon get used to the new situation. So it's not too difficult to adjust.

Were you at the wedding? Did you come to the house afterwards?

I was around on the day, taking an interest, passing the time with the others (referring to other members of the family also in the spirit world) like we would have been if we'd been there. It's just like that, you know. It's natural. We were just there chatting away like we would have been anyway. The only difference is you can't see us and we can't chat with you.

I saw three gold lights when I arrived home that night.

Yes, well, that was us.

* * *

After one of our spirit visitors had left, a member of our circle commented that it was very interesting that the guest speakers took the time and trouble to come through to talk to us. Hai replied:

They demonstrate for you the closeness of the two worlds and the interpenetrating nature of them. They are like two gloves on different hands.

So the spirit world actually surrounds the earth, does it?

Just so, or the earth surrounds the spirit world, depending on your point of view. Which would be again another interesting debate for your duality concept!

Chapter 11

Johanson

One night a spirit came through who claimed that he and a member of the Home Circle had once shared a life together in Sweden as husband and wife. As often is the case, much of the communication was personal and about that life; however, it also touched upon the topic of reincarnation, the nature of human relationships and how to reach out to your guides. The main message running through the communication was: If you love someone you will be happy to let them return to the physical plane.

Johanson's Message:
If you really love, you can let go

The person in question asked:
Was our life together a long time ago?
Ah, not so long ago. A long time ago for you now, perhaps, but from our vantage point it is not long at all.
A hundred years?
Ah, you want me to do the mathematics. Well, it's not so easy.
Is this the first time you've come through like this?
It's the first time I've tried this way, yes (through trance mediumship.) This way is not so easy at times. We shared many times together, happy times, very happy times.
Do you have a reason for coming through now?
Yes, to make your acquaintance again, to celebrate our happy times together.

Another member of the group asked:

Did you miss her when she returned (to earth)?

Oh yes! But we all must move on our way at times. We must have the strength and the love to let go. If you cannot let go you have not great love. We must all learn to let go when the time is right.

Will she remember you when she passes to spirit? Will it take some time before she remembers?

She will remember quite quickly.

Is her personality similar now to that of her previous life?

In some ways, perhaps a little more—no, I shouldn't say that. We all change a little when we come back, because we all need different experiences. It wouldn't do to come back with the same identical personality as we had the last time, or the time before. You were a little freer, shall we say, a little more—how you say—free and easy.

Do we come back with the same energy?

You have an essence of your person, of your spiritual self, your spiritual being, but this may express itself in different forms. It's like if you fill different flexible containers with water. They'd take different shapes, but the water is water just the same.

You adapt to the shape that you need to be for that lifetime, then?

You rather take on a shape, which you need to have for that lifetime. It fits and it serves you well for that purpose, for that time.

Will you incarnate again? Will you be able to decide?

I will. I will be able to decide, yes.

So you don't have to if you don't want to?

No; not in my case.

We don't all get the choice?

It depends upon our circumstance, upon what you call karma also. But within limits we may choose if we wish to come. We may have guidance in this at times from wiser souls.

Is the purpose so that you can develop and go on to a higher realm?

The purpose is to discover ourselves, or to re-discover ourselves. It is to recognise ourselves, to grow closer to ourselves, and whatever realm you are in, in the spirit world, you have recognised yourself. If you know yourself truly you know the Great Spirit, the Great Mind also. So the realm you are in doesn't matter, because you know yourself and you're at peace with yourself. And this is partly the meaning of the lady's meditation tonight (Isleen had taken us through a meditation earlier in the evening) that you may know peace within yourself when you know your spiritual essence, spiritual being.

The plane you are living on now, is it for you very happy?

It is very happy, very happy. (Johansen continued repeating these words to emphasise the point)

Do you still live on a farm or do you have a house?

No, we don't need this, but we live in what you would call the countryside, because this is where we are happiest. It's where we are most comfortable.

Do you live with your family now?

We live together with a group of friends, some of them *you* know.

Do you have animals?

The animals are all around us, but they are free to come and go and they sometimes choose to stay to pass some time with us.

Johansen explained that relationships change from one incarnation to another; however, it is the *love* between souls, which is important. Jane asked:

Were I and (another member of the Home Circle) brother and sister in a previous life? We've been told by a medium that we are.

Not in the life I speak of, but I believe you were in another incarnation. But you see these relationships, which we bond between us, can change from one lifetime to the next. They are not important themselves. What is important is the love that flows between us and which bonds us together in a more durable way than any of these relationships of which we speak. The bond of love surpasses the particular love of husband and wife, of brother and sister, and so on. The bond of love is a deep bond whatever the relationship, however it manifests in a particular lifetime.

So it doesn't matter about the relationship?

No, the bond of love is not lessened because the relationship is different.

Do we sometimes come back with the same people but in different relationships?

This is possible, but it is not necessarily always so. It does not need to be so, but it can happen.

Someone else asked:

Did Jane, move on to another plane before she reincarnated?

We spent some time together within the spiritual planes before she reincarnated. She had a need to be reincarnated. And though there was some sadness to the parting we were glad for her, because we knew that it had to be. It was in her interest. It was a need, which had to be met.

Does the time she has been away seem to be a long time to you?

It seems a short time because, as you know, time has little concept for us here.

So it's just like she's nipped out to the shops?

Yes, (he smiled) but I'm not sure what she will buy to bring back.

She won't be the same person when she comes back, will she?

She will grow—she will grow.

When you die do you automatically go to a place, which resembles earth, or can you choose?

You may choose where you wish to live in the spirit planes, within reason. And therefore you may choose an area that resembles the countryside to which you were used to on the earth plane. But it's only a similarity to a point, because the lands of the spirit world are more refined; more in harmony; are not polluted like your lands; are not distorted by your creations, by your buildings, your roads and so forth; so they are more natural, more beautiful. They are more real in many ways and so we may choose where we wish to reside within reason.

If the spirit world borders the earth plane, where does pollution end?

There are no borders; they interpenetrate. How can pollution affect us? We merely feel the vibration though, of the pain, which your pollution brings. But we are not directly affected by it in our world. Only if we sense the vibration, pain, discomfort, which is created for you.

Jane had another question:

Can you connect with me on the earth plane even though I have no conscious memory of you?

I can connect with you. We don't have a problem in seeing you all. We have our spiritual eyes with which we can look, so there is no problem with this. So we can indeed link, can indeed visit and see you in your new life, and we wish you well.

When you do see us, is it our etheric bodies you see or our physical bodies?
We can see your physical.
Is that a form of mediumship, then, the way you see us?
When you speak of mediumship it's a bit confusing, because we see what we see. We can relate to the vibration. There is no need for mediumship and indeed when you speak of it on your plane it's a bit inaccurate at times, because what you speak of is rather a heightened sensitivity to the spiritual vibration. The faculty is there for you to develop and you are able to see when it's developed to the right point. There is nothing special about it, is what I mean. It's natural. Some may have a heightened sensitivity, a heightened awareness, a more developed ability to see, but the seeing is inherent in all to a degree. Our worlds are natural. They interpenetrate each other and even this is not accurate because if I talk of interpenetrating each other you conjure up an image perhaps of two worlds and there are no two worlds. There is One Reality as you have been told many times.
I've been praying recently to be able to connect with my spirit guide, because I understand it helps the guide as well as me. I'm not sure I'm being heard.
If you reach out you will connect. There is no fear of not connecting. You cannot end up talking to yourself; you should be so lucky. There is always someone to listen. It is important to reach out to the right ones though. There are always ears ready to listen; some you would rather went on their way without listening. But if you reach out for the good, the true, the loving spirits, they will listen and they will respond. They will help you even though you may not sense them at times. They will help you.
Can they read our thoughts or do we need to say the prayers out loud?
If you reach out with your thoughts to them they can read them. But you must reach out. We cannot intrude upon your thoughts. But if you reach out with your thoughts you will bring the gateway, because you have opened the gateway willingly by reaching out.
Is it easier for the spirit world if we speak?
No, it's just as easy if you reach out with your thoughts, your loving thoughts.
I must now bid you farewell. I am most happy to have met you all and I wish you all well. I wish you the peace of which the lady (Isleen) spoke to you, a deep peace which cannot be surpassed. I wish you

peace and I bid you farewell. Who knows we may have an opportunity to speak again. You have a rather long queue of people but we will see.

Thank you for persisting. We know it was difficult for you to come through.

I thank you. It is not always easy from our side. People do not always appreciate this, but it does require effort and persistence at times. I thank you for your recognition and I bid you a loving farewell. Goodbye to you.

*   *   *

Following Johansson's visit, one member of our group asked Hai about the communication.

I wondered why his wife had returned to earth and he had remained in the spirit world. Was this because Jane wanted to learn more?

It was a time that was ripe for her to come forward to the earth plane again. There is no problem with this. We are all growing, we are all walking our own path, albeit with the support and love of others along the way, but we have our own path to tread, our own development to seek.

He said that when his wife came back to the earth plane he could let her go because he loved her.

This is true, and so even we on the spirit side of life, can learn from letting go. There is a One Reality as we keep saying, an Oneness. It is truly a One Reality.

Chapter 12

Bobby: Henry: Harriet

We have included Henry Bobby and Harriet in this book because we feel that all three communications, demonstrate how, not only our strengths, but our weakness too can be valuable learning experiences whilst we are on the earth plane.

Bobby told us that he'd been known as Robert in his last incarnation. However, he was such a serious person that it prevented him from enjoying his life; therefore, when he passed over to spirit he discovered that he needed to "lighten up." In order to achieve this, one of the first things he was encouraged to do was to take on the name Bobby, Nevertheless, Bobby amply demonstrates how his "weakness" was also strength. He told us: We need to keep a balance in our lives.

Henry was a little different. He told us that he was a placid person in his last incarnation and would often offer advice to people who had relationship difficulties. Henry's communication shows us how our experiences, when on the earth plane, can be put to good use when we pass to the spirit world.

Henry also demonstrates how giving to others actually helps his own development.

Harriet, we will explain in some detail, later.

Bobby
The Message:
We always learn something, no matter which road we take

Bobby began the communication with:

You are most welcome and you would welcome me, I am sure. It's so pleasant to make your acquaintance. My name is Bobby. It wasn't

Bobby when I was on the earthly plane. It was Robert but I've taken the name of Bobby because I was a serious so-and-so when I was on the earthly plane and to take the name of Bobby is a vehicle, reminder, of my seriousness of my earthly life, that I'm trying to remedy in my present situation.

So the name Bobby sounds more light-hearted?

This is so. This is just the case.

Have you found it easy or difficult to become more light-hearted?

I am learning. The environment, the company is conducive to this learning and therefore I am learning but there are those who cajole me, who engage merriment with me to bring me to this path.

They are teaching you to be more light-hearted, then?

They teach me in a light-hearted way by their company, their presence and their—banter will have to do for a word, for I cannot find an appropriate word.

Do you prefer this?

I'm enjoying it immensely as I enter into its spirit.

Was there a reason why you were so serious?

I was overtaken by my environment, my circumstances. I lost hold of the rudder and the environment became the rudder, took the rudder. You see my meaning. A dangerous circumstance to allow to come about, for we must retain the mastership of our own "vessel."

Did you become very depressed with your situation?

Not so much depressed as absorbed; unbalanced, out of kilter.

If you saw something funny would you laugh at it?

There were indeed moments of merriment; moments where I could regain some of my composure but these were rare in comparison with what they should have been.

Was life worrying for you?

It was serious rather than worrying. It was a serious business for me. But if you view life in this way you lose life. Life should be merriment, at its heart, at its essence be merriment. This is often not the way of the world, of course. It's not our individual fault to any great extent sometimes when we're overtaken by the way of the world but it's not to our benefit, it's not good for our health to allow this to occur, to take it too seriously. We must crack the joke in the face of the serious world. There are times, of course, to be serious. It would not be fitting to laugh at a time of distress, of discomfort for someone. But to take my meaning at its heart, life should be a smile, merriment to see us through.

Do you do a job in spirit that is light-hearted?

My job is set for me to be light-hearted, to bring merriment. Now that is a job, a task indeed, is it not, for someone who had lost his sense of merriment. To bring merriment to others; can you imagine a harder task, a harder job?

And how long have you been in the spirit world?

It seems for an eternity but I do make progress.

When you were on the earth plane, was it the only way you could get through life by adopting a serious attitude?

It is indeed a survival tactic for some, to absorb themselves in the world; to sense an enemy around every corner and to plan for meeting them with the appropriate tactics. But this is a paranoid mentality. It's not conducive to ease of mind, to ease of temper, to peace of mind in any form. You must trust in the benevolence, of providence of life more while doing our bit, by making provision as best we may, according to our needs but without becoming obsessive about concerns for the future or concerns about our present circumstances and environment.

So what did you learn on the earth plane from all that? Was it simply that you must not take life seriously or did you learn more than that?

I learnt strength, for though my path was in error in some respects, I learnt strength in facing this path. And so, you see, it is often the way that even an infirmity, or a weakness in us, in our character, in our response to our situations can be a strength in another way, do you follow me? In that I met my circumstances, my environment with steadfastness and with resoluteness and from that point of view, even though it was a weakness, it built up a strength in me. But it would have been a far greater measure, far greater benefit, positiveness if I'd been able to marry this resoluteness, this steadfastness of character with merriment. A balance of positives, you understand.

And so although it hasn't been a wasted life by any means, for it has brought about strength in some measure, in it's own form, in it's own way, what I must do now is balance this strength with another form of strength and more importantly, to balance it with strength of insight of the nature of life, of living; which, in its essence, is loving, is compassionate, is hopeful, is optimistic, is creative. It is these things that I must now learn, which I must now develop in greater measure.

Trust in life. We must develop a trust in life, for all things will work out ultimately.

So did you take the wrong path really in life, not the path you were meant to take?

The path we are meant to take; ah now, there, my friend, is the rub; the path we are meant to take. And how many of us take this path we are meant to take?

I'm not sure that we truly know what the path is.

Well I will tell you, my friend—

Bobby told us a story to demonstrate his point.

You may set out along the road to Peking—yes? You set along the road to Peking and you say to yourself, I am going to Peking. But there are so many avenues branching off this road to Peking, so many attractive sideshows to visit; so many pedlars of wares to entice you (laughs) down the avenues, pointing the way to their goods, their sparkling entanglements and so, my friend, you see the path we are meant to tread. Now I would say to you, although we set out and say to ourselves, we will walk the road to Peking, perhaps walking the road to Peking inevitably takes in the side shows. You take my meaning?

Now the thing about this, is that all things can be turned to good. You like your catechisms but the catechisms become a bit worn with age and use. This is the reality. And so though my life from one perspective couldn't be described as ideal, for, as I have told you, it lacked balance. In particular it lacked positivity, merriment, understanding of the essence of all life, of the beauty of life, the need to trust life, the need to love life. Though it lacked these positives and therefore lacked the balance that these positives bring. I, nevertheless, learned much and gained a degree, a type of strength, by my own response to situations that can be turned to good, which can be built upon so they are not wasted. It is a pity I couldn't achieve the balance in my earthly life but we may continue "our walk to Peking" and achieve the balance at other times in other ways.

Will you return to earth?

I may but I may learn more here. I may learn what I need to learn here. But we may revisit our earthly haunts. We shall see in the fullness of time; we shall see.

*   *   *

Eileen said it was time to finish and Bobby gave us his blessing.

Yes, so we'll be on our way and we wish you to have a mind not to become worn down. We wish you to have a mind not to fall into a rut, a six-foot rut, where you cannot see above the rim and feel you are trammelled down this rut, which you must follow inexorably. We wish you to have a mind to this. We wish you to have a mind to look for a rock while you are walking along this rut. That you may put this rock firmly and squarely in the middle and stand on top of it and peek above the horizon to see the grand vista beyond. To see the other paths, which may be trod, which may be more pleasing and offer more balance and peace of mind to you. This we wish for you, my friends. Please keep in mind this image I give to you when you feel trammelled, when you feel oppressed, dragged down, worn down. When you feel you are in danger of mechanically following a path, when you feel you are slipping into a rut; keep this image in mind before you please and my story also and stand on your rock to peak above and look at the horizons beyond. Goodbye, my friends. Perhaps we will have occasion to talk again in the future. Goodbye.

Henry
The Message:
Relationships still have to be worked on, even in the Spirit World

Henry came through with a strong American accent but when we asked him where he had lived when on the earth plane he said he couldn't remember. Henry said he might remember as we got talking. He also said he'd been in the spirit world a very long time; so long that he could no longer clearly remember what it was like on the earth plane. He eventually remembered that he'd been a farmer out on the planes. Although he now lives in what he described as "the mountains" he told us that he had lots of folk who visited him and said they seemed to want to come and talk to him and usually went away feeling pretty satisfied.

We asked Henry:

What kind of things do you talk to these people about, Henry?
All kinds of things. We talk about relationships sometimes. Relationships are tricky things, aren't they?
Even in the spirit world?
Oh yeah, don't you kid yourself, Helen. They can be tricky things here too.
I thought that when we came there it would be peaceful?
It is mighty peaceful compared to what you enjoy sometimes, that's a fact. But don't you kid yourself—you still gotta work at it. But a lot of things work for you while you're working at it.

Another circle member asked:
I thought you were automatically drawn to a place where you do get on with people.
You are drawn to your place; you're drawn to those folk whom you feel at ease with. But can you honestly tell me, young lady, that when you're surrounded by folk you are pleased with and you love and you enjoy that there's no time that you don't have a wrangle with them.
Yes, you're right.
Well then it would get mighty boring if we were all floating around smiling or grinning from ear to ear with each other.
So you have to have a ding-dong sometimes, do you?
You do, you do, to learn, to learn your place.
So are you a relationship advisor?
Well, I wouldn't call myself that and I wouldn't have seen myself like that but I guess some of what I do is about that.
So that is the role you have been manoeuvred into, is it?
Yes, and with a beard.
Oh, you have a beard, do you?
I have a beard, which I hung onto, if you know what I mean.
You mean you have created one for yourself?

I have. I've got this picture of myself that I project out to the folks around me. I guess I could project myself as an agony aunt if I wanted to. (Laughter)

How did you get your experience to help others with their relationship difficulties?

Well I had a big family. I had a lot of folks around me and I was of a peaceable inclination. But some were not and I learned a lot by observing them, interacting with them and trying to advise them; trying to establish the peace between them and so on. I've got a lot of battle scars, which I guess I have learned a lot from. But you know when you're an observer, a passer-by, sort of, in these conflicts, you get a scar as other folks do; (laughing) you can't just put your armour on and switch off.

So you felt some of the pain, did you?

So I felt some of the pain and I got some of the pain 'cause you start putting your oar in, someone's likely to break it for you if they don't like what you say; but still you do what you can.

Do you enjoy the role?

I do. It comes naturally to me, as you can imagine.

You like to send people away peaceful, do you?

I try. Not that there's conflict here in the way that you would expect conflict in your world but there can be misunderstandings. There can be deceptions or different points of view so I get in the middle of it and do what I can. You gotta be sort of philosophical about all this. Laid back, calm and just talk folk through it and say well, yeah, I can see your point of view but do you think if we looked at it this way we could see something of how this chap, this guy, this lady is seeing it? "Why would I want to do that?" they might say but I say well, it might be just a good idea to try, to give it a try.

How are they attracted to you? Do you send out your loving thoughts to them?

Well, yeah, I do but, you know, it's not so much that I have to send out loving thoughts—it's because it's like my vibration seems to attract them, you see. Bit like; not quite the same but a bit like one of your lighthouses on a headland. People are just aware of the light. But with me, I guess it's more that the people sort of *feel* something, feel drawn to it. It's a bit like a "feeling energy" beaming out; rather than light. You understand me?

Do you mean like a magnet?

Yeah well, they know, they feel this sort of wave, this sort of pulse and think (laughing) well I could do with some of that.

Like comforting waves?

Yea, but you know we work the other way too, because when they start to come to me I can sense them and I think, oh I could do with some of that. I could help that person, yeah, and I look forward to them. I can *feel* them coming and I look forward to them and we get down together and talk things through. I like to get to know new folk. It's always nice to meet new folk. You know it's like if you went down to a riverbed or something and you were picking through the stones, yeah, and every now and then you might find something that's shiny and beautiful, shiny pebble or stone. It's a bit like that when these folks come to me. It's a bit like turning up a bright shiny pebble on the riverbed: a beautiful thing to happen, to see.

Is that how things work in the spirit world? If someone has a problem do they attune to a certain vibration to get help?

Yeah, they know, they can feel the vibrations. It's a bit like—if I give you another analogy—It's a bit like an old honeybee, floating around in the air, on his wings, yeah. He smells the scents from a hundred flowers but he knows the one he needs, the one he's attracted to the strongest. So that's another good way to look at this, yeah. The flower knows too that he's heading for him; flower sends out his scent for he knows there's gonna be some little bumble bee folks turning up.

Do you think you will ever change from your present vibration?

I'm sure; I'm told that it will happen some day. Some day being a manner of speaking, of course, but yes some day this could be. But I'm content at the moment. Content with what I'm doing, what I'm being and what I'm experiencing. It's mighty good, mighty good.

      *   *   *

Henry was asked if he would come back to earth and he indicated that he was open to the possibility. He said he lived on his own because he had more freedom to do what he wanted to do. Nevertheless he keeps in touch with his family. He finished the communication with these comforting words:

Well, I'm might pleased to have met you folk and I truly wish you well. But it is truly a beautiful place up here. You got nothing to fear. It is truly a beautiful place. It's like the best of what you can see around you but a hundred million times better. So I'll be on my way.

Harriet

And then there was Harriet: Words cannot adequately convey Harriet's light-hearted banter. Her cheerful sing-song voice and her delightful, carefree way of looking at life, both now and when she was last on earth. She describes herself as a "feather" floating in and out. It was clear from her banter that she'd lived during a time when the monarch of the day would hold regular "get togethers" or Balls and it was clear that Harriet had been a regular guest at these Balls.

Harriet loved to socialise and chat with people. She told us that her favourite activity had been to listen in on people's conversations, collect lots of information then drop it where it would cause the most disruption. In fact, Isleen, another member of our spirit group, confirmed later that, Harriet had been obliged to, make a certain amount of adjustment when she reached the spirit world.

On Harriet's second visit to our group, she was asked what she's doing now in the spirit world. She indicates that she's "networking" but doesn't clarify what she means. It wasn't until her third visit to us that we discovered that she's now putting her "skills" into positive use by using them to put people in the spirit world in contact with each other.

Harriet's experience shows how skills, even when used in a non-constructive way when here on earth, can nonetheless be put to positive use upon reaching the spirit world.

The following is a short extract of her second visit. As with Davia's communications, it is difficult to give an accurate flavour of Harriet's repartee without hearing it for yourself. She was in "top" form so the session was particularly funny. Harriet certainly raised the energies in our room that night.

Harriet began the conversation by saying:

We have met before. I am Harriet.

I thought it was you, Harriet.
You did. What was it that gave me away?
It was the tone of your voice and your laugh.
Oh my laugh gives me away again. Is there no secret that I can keep?
No, not with us.

No, and you have your contraption to help you (the mini disc.) I would have given an arm to have such a contraption in my day. What I could have done with such a contraption. Oh yes, it would have been a great asset at my tea parties, carefully concealed. (Laughter) What a delight it would have been.

You weren't a mischief-maker were you, Harriet?
Only a little.
Sounds like you were a bit of a naughty girl to me, Harriet. (Laughter)

Well we had to have some fun, didn't we? You have to have some fun, don't you? Which is why I've come through tonight to give you a little bit of fun after our serious Egyptian friend (our previous visitor) who is most wise, most wise but grave somewhat.

So your feather drifted our way again did it, Harriet?
You remembered?
I did, of course.
I am most gratified, most gratified.
Did we ask you who was on the throne when you were on earth?
(Laughter) I was going to say it depended on the time of day.
I mean the sovereign.

Well I was fortunate in having many sovereigns. (More laughter) My husband was well endowed with sovereigns.

So was he very generous, then?

Oh yes, indeed, he was most generous. I wouldn't take any issue with him over that; most generous He needed a little guidance of course, in how to be generous at times and how to spend his money but he was generous.

But no doubt you were very skilled in that, Harriet?
Tactful I'd say, Eileen.
Did you meet the reigning monarch of the day?

The jokes continued:

You will not give up, will you? The reigning monarch; is this the monarch who stands in the rain? (Laughter) yes I think his name was George.

Did you go to court?

No in spite of all my misdemeanours, I did not find myself in court.

Did you go to King George's court, Harriet?

I did indeed, oh yes, and I took part in the Balls.

But did you have fun?

Oh I had fun, most certainly fun. Fun in full measure and it was amazing what you could pick up.

In the form of gossip, you mean?

Yes, I was thinking of the gossip but it was amazing what you could pick up just listening in, quietly and carefully, in the right places, in the right quarters, behind the backs of the right people.

One member of the group commented that she was usually oblivious to others' conversations. Harriet answered:

Oh what a waste, what a waste, yes you should not be oblivious. You need, of course, to *appear* to be oblivious; so this is one of the skills I will leave with you tonight. You must *appear* to be oblivious, appear to all the world that you have not the *slightest* concern with what is being said around you but you are, in fact, "all ears" and (laughs) the more you have the better and indeed this is another part of the skill, you see. We are endowed unfortunately with only two ears, are we not, so we have to compensate for this by usefully employing the ears of others and putting them to good purpose and, of course, you must gather in this intelligence to use to great effect. Yes, old George had his spies, you know, but the truth of it is that what **we** did not know was not worth knowing and we knew a considerable amount more than his spies.

Did you like the dressing up and ceremony?

Oh yes, yes the Balls the events were an invigorating experience; full of colour and gaiety and the music was so light and beautiful. We had a joyous time.

What do you actually do in the spirit world now, Harriet?

I network, yes, and there is so much scope for networking here, you know, so much scope; oh absolutely. Yes we can network and not only to our own realm but we can network to other realms and we can network to other levels of the spirit lands. The possibilities are endless; you would be amazed, absolutely amazed.

How does it work, then?

Well now (laugh) that would be giving my secrets away, wouldn't it? That's worth far more than the name of old Georgie boy.

Sounds like you have hours of fun with all this, Harriet.

Harriet laughed again and responded:

Well what is the good of life if you cannot have fun? Not a lot of point, is there? You have so many serious people around you today in your world, I mean so many serious people. Oh they go round with their hanging mouths, their stern faces, deep thoughts of gravity, yes, must not forget the deep thoughts of gravity, yes so serious and yet old Davia might come along with his oar and give them a nudge and before they know were they are, they are in the spirit land and where is all their seriousness then? What good will all their serious thoughts do them then? They will have to lighten up or they will become an interminable bore to us.

It's probably worrying about what happens to them when they die that make them serious.

Well, what a paradox.

Do you dance in the spirit world? Do you still have your Balls, Harriet?

Oh yes, we have our dances; oh we have our dances. They are beautiful things absolutely.

Did you have Father Christmas, when on the earth plane?

Yes we had St Nicholas, an occasion for my husband to deliver of his generosity with my guidance on how best to employ themselves.

I will have to float off now and hope, my dear friends, to talk to you again in the future.

Chapter 13

Royalty

Mary, Elizabeth & Ted

The Message:
The Curse of Fear

Mary Queen of Scots and Elizabeth the 1st communicated within a few weeks of each other. We spoke to Mary first: Elizabeth later indicated that she wanted to tell us her view of the situation. History has shown that the relationship between the two was extremely complex and ended in Elizabeth's decision to end Mary's life.

Mary indicated that she is now enjoying the peace which she never had while in her last incarnation but it is clear that even after all this time she has not been able to forgive Elizabeth.

Elizabeth described to us the difficulties of being a monarch in her day. She comments on the future of the English monarchy, tells us what she has learnt from her life as the Queen of England and the lessons she learnt from her relationship with Mary.

One of our group members sensed Mary clairvoyantly, before she came through. The questions were asked by a variety of people within the group.

It is interesting to note the difference in the opening words from each monarch and how their different personalities are demonstrated in these communications.

*　　　　　*　　　　　*

Mary Queen of Scots

Mary began the communication with:

I would wish to speak to you and I must ask your permission because of my situation now. But my situation of the past would not have required it, would not have needed to ask permission from anyone. I am who the gentleman says I am.

Are you Mary Queen of Scots?

I am indeed. You have attuned to me well, sir. I thank you for that. I thank you for making the link. (Mary smiles and continues) It is difficult in my headless condition.

I take it you are not that way now?

No, I am not that way now as you say quite rightly. I am whole again, ah yes, whole again.

There are lots of books, which say there have been sightings of you in castles and suchlike, so are you fully in the spirit world?

I have put in an appearance from time to time but I have not been trapped in those conditions. I enter freely into them when I choose to make my appearance. I frequented these places for a considerable time as you well know and therefore I built up an affinity with them. I visited them from time to time like you would your home when you have finished with your earth body. You, Eileen, have visited one of my haunts in Edinburgh when your child was little.

Yes, it was a lovely place. Do you have a special purpose in coming back to these places?

You have afinity to these places and you wish to revisit them. You would wish to visit a favourite place again on your earthly journey. You do visit places, do you not, that you are fond of and it is the same for us. We visit those places, which we are fond of on the earthly realm and we enjoy our visit though it may awaken painful memories sometimes. But this is the nature of life, is it not, that places may gender great happiness, great memories of happiness in us but may also engender painful memories and painful emotions. It is the nature of life, is it not, and we must bear it as best we can, it is a paradox.

Do you live in a palace in the spirit world?

I do not live in a palace in the way of the palaces that I lived in on the earthly plane but I am comfortable in my house, which is an expansive house and suitable for my purpose because I like to entertain people and my house is conducive to this purpose.

Did you find it easy or difficult to adjust when you passed over?

I found it quite easy to adjust because my life had become difficult on this side. It was not too difficult to make the transition.

Were you able to forgive Elizabeth?

It was—it was and is hard to forgive what she did.

These people who you entertain in your house—are they people you associated with on the earth plane or are they new friends?

Some of them are people who I was acquainted with on the earthly journey, but there were others, whom I have associated with since coming to my place here. We have no limitations upon how many people we may associate with and we meet many people, many interesting people of many different backgrounds and skills.

Do you in turn get invited to such gatherings?

We do—we do indeed. We meet others in their own abodes and in the places where we gather within the "hubbub." Your word has entered our dictionary. (There'd been much amusement from our spirit friends when a group member first used the word. They now use it regularly)

Do you remember living in this part of the country (North West) when you were on the earth plane?

I lived in many parts of the countryside because I was moved around a lot when I was alive on your plane. I was moved around a lot from place to place, which was troublesome to me but which served a purpose for them. For moving me around meant there was less likelihood of focus of activity around me.

With all the experiences you had on the earth plane, is there a particular piece of advice you could give us to help with our own lives?

With great power goes great loneliness. Your friends are few, the friends who you can trust are fewer and friendship for those who are in power is a precious gift indeed, a precious gift to be cherished, for it is a gift of great rarity.

Did you feel very alone, then, for the majority of your life?

There was a pause; Mary replied:

I have felt very alone particularly in the latter years for there are those who do not want to know what you would call, I believe, a loser. But also there are those who want to know you for what they can get themselves, for how you will serve their ends—how they may use you to serve their ends but without a care for your welfare, without a care for the outcome, for you.

When you made the transition from the earth world to spirit, was there a special friend who came to you to help?

Yes, there was one who had become a friend on the earth plane and who had gone on before me. He met me when I passed over. This was a great comfort and I would wish you all such comfort at your time.

Should you have been the Queen of England?

Yes, and Scotland, but it was not meant to be.

Have you been in the spirit world ever since?

I have been in the spirit ever since that time. I have not been back. If you had, experienced such a traumatic life as mine you would not be in any great hurry to come back and you need time to adjust to take things in to recharge, to revitalise.

To us, that is quite a piece of time and I was wondering if you have moved from the realm where you started?

I have not moved beyond the realm where I started in on my passing, for I am comfortable here and at my ease and at peace and this is most welcome. I have no desire to move on at the moment, for I am content and at peace.

I must ask you this question: have you been to the Halls of Learning? (Most of our visitors during this time were asked this question)

I have been to the Halls of Learning and held the Pearl of Great Wisdom.

Is it a place you go to often?

I frequent it regularly, for there is much wisdom and knowledge to be gleaned there and it is food for the soul.

And with the particular difficulties of your earthly life, has it helped you in some ways?

It has indeed been of help as it has been of help to speak to those who would speak with me, who would discuss my affairs, who would discuss my experiences. All these things are most helpful to readjust to the reality.

Have you met your father since passing over, Mary?

I have. He was not a bad-hearted man, you know, in his essence. He was like a child, a misguided and unruly child, but such power in the hands of a misguided and unruly child is danger indeed. And it may turn the unruly child to a tyrant. He had some hard lessons to learn.

What makes you laugh, Mary?

In truth I seek and enjoy peace and contentment more than laughter, for the peace is the peace I sorely missed and was without on your plane.

Can you tell us your thoughts on the monarchy now?

Your times have changed and while there was need of us and our like in the days gone by, to pull, to meld the people together, you have no need of figureheads such as us in your day. You have all moved on, you have all changed. You have all "come of age;" therefore, you need to create your form of government appropriate to your wishes and needs.

The monarchy doesn't have the same control anymore but it is outdated.

Yes it is outdated and you will move it on.

Do you think this will happen in my lifetime, Mary?

It will take a bit longer than that but it will come.

Are you still known as Mary in the spirit world?

I am known as Mary and there are those who use another word, another name for me, who are intimate to me.

I must leave you now. I would thank you for your indulgence, I have found your conversation most pleasant, and I would wish you well with your endeavours.

*   *   *

We spoke to Hai the following night about Mary's visit and one member expressed surprise that she was still on the same level in the spirit world. Hai answered:

She is still on a developmental journey. We are all on a developmental journey but she has a journey very much linked to her last life.

Does she actually choose to stay? She said she was at peace?

She has a need to stay and this need is recognized and is gone along with because she has a need to remain on this level to enable her to readjust, to take stock, to reflect upon her life experiences and she had a lot of life experiences in her last life. Therefore, she has a great need to reflect upon these, to achieve a harmony over them, to achieve an acceptance over them to enable her to reach a calm peace of mind within her centre, so that she may move on.

How do you measure that in time?

We do not measure it in time for time here is of no consequence or any meaning so we do not measure it in time. Time is the need of the soul here. If the soul has great need it will spend longer in a realm of adjustment. We have no measure of time; we impose no markers of time.

*   *   *

Queen Elizabeth the 1st

She began with:

I have deigned to come to you. I have deigned to come to you. You spoke to my cousin some time ago and now I wish to make my point of view known to you. I am Elizabeth.

So you want to tell us how you felt about it all, do you?

I wish to make known my opinion, my perspective on events. For the events were not without their difficulties, for the times were most difficult. The Spaniards were at our doors. The Scots were at our doors. The Irish were at our doors. I had to protect the realm. Intrigue and treason and it was not easy to achieve this. Rulers' decisions are sometimes boxed in like an alley, nowhere to go—most difficult to achieve for the benefit of all.

Did you ever think of marriage to make an alliance as a way to make yourself stronger?

I did not wish to be second fiddle to any man. I had my own mind and my own will and my own knowing what needed to be done. I had my comforts in the men way, I mean.

What kind of a childhood did you have, Elizabeth?

A tumultuous one: A tumultuous one. Times were difficult; my father chopping and changing all the time; chopping and changing. It was most sad what she had to put up with. (We understood she was referring to Catherine of Aragon) Broke her heart to be put aside like some worthless trollop.

Have you seen your father since you've been in the spirit world?

I have and I have made my mind known to him clearly in a way that would have not gone down well while on the earthly plane, daughter or no. I would not have risked the encounter.

Has he changed now?

He has learnt the error of his ways and is moderated.

And you have seen Mary again?

I have but she does not see my way yet. She does not see my way for what I did.

Do you get invited to her functions?

We meet but we do not meet socially.

What do you do now in the spirit world?

I like the arts. I develop my artistic skills.

Are you still a very forthright person in the spirit world?

I am forthright. I believe it is the way to be—forthright—to make your mind clear to those around you—to engage them in directness.

I am of similar mind myself but I have to be careful because I am not a queen.

It is a problem when you *are* Queen. You try to engage those in directness but they shift and they weave and they dodge. Give you what you want to hear, rather than what you wish them to say—to be direct.

I would guess that it is similar now except, perhaps, not so dangerous for our Queen or the Royal family?

Oh yes, where there is power this will be the problem, that people will not speak their minds, for they fear the power and will not speak their minds against it lest they have repercussions upon their own fate.

Are you aware that Princess Margaret died recently?

Yes, (Elizabeth was still reminiscing about the monarchy) but these are pretend monarchs are they not. They have no power and no responsibility of the like which we had to meet.

I suppose you would have had the role of both the Queen and Prime Minister, would you?

We had advisors but we had to make the decision in the final analysis.

Do you think there is a role for the monarchy in the future?

I do not. There is no point in having "pretend" monarchs.

Did you find it difficult to adjust to the spirit world?

It was difficult to adjust, for I was accustomed to a certain standard of life, a way of life—conditioned to having those wait around and this was not to be and so it was difficult at first. It was difficult.

Do you know why you chose to return to the earth plane as Queen of England? Was there a particular experience you wanted from that?

Yes—yes, to have the responsibility for a nation.

Were you satisfied at the end how you had managed that?

It was not as I expected. I was so hemmed in on all sides—thought I would have freedom to do as I thought best but we were hemmed in on all sides. Our decisions were shackled to the lead weights, which others had, which others had given us. Power is limited where others have their own power and influence and play their dark games in the shadows.

Are there any things that you wished you had done differently?

It is no use thinking about what might have been, for we try to make the best of our decisions when they are called for. What transpires—transpires. I would have preferred not to have taken certain actions but at the time I felt there was no alternative.

You've certainly gone down in history as being a very strong monarch a valuable monarch, Elizabeth.

I fought for the interests of the country and achieved some success in this I believe.

Did you have someone with you when you passed over into the spirit world that you cared about and were close to?

I had a friend, a counsellor.

And did you meet up with your mother?

Yes.

From a Monarch's point of view, would you say that only correct decisions can be made through knowledge and wisdom?

Knowledge and wisdom are invaluable to be sure, but it is very difficult to make good decisions even with knowledge and wisdom, for, as I have said, you are hemmed in, shackled. It is not easy to find the best way forward and some decisions sometimes seem not to be decisions at all because circumstance happenstance, push, the decision in a certain direction. We are not as free as we would have ourselves believe we are free and this is a great difficulty.

Did you find that you had to use, an almost, stepping-stone approach, to make things happen how you ultimately wanted it to be?

Manoeuvring, you mean? We had to manoeuvre at times, to out-manoeuvre those who were manoeuvring against us—a game of chess.

Do you think you benefited, as you originally set out to do, from the decisions to take the road that you did?

I learnt from it. I developed from it. I achieved more potential from it so, for this, I must be thankful. But I carry a heavy burden for it as well, for the decisions that I had to take, and which are still bearing their consequences.

What would happen to someone who gave you advice that you trusted but in fact was only interested in self? Would they carry a heavier burden for misleading you in a particular way?

They would carry a burden for being full of their own self-interest and therefore their karma would be attached to this, for where our own self-interest prevails we have not the good of the many at heart. And where we have not the good of many at heart we enkindle karma for ourselves, which must be paid at some point in the future.

Did you have difficulty yourself in making decisions for the best of all, Elizabeth?

I made decisions for the good of the country but the good of the country was sometimes in my interests too and so the two become entangled and difficult to disentangle. And I, like others, have got caught up in this dilemma at times, being unable to disentangle my own self-interest from the interest of the country.

Did you find it very, very, difficult to have Mary put to death?

It was difficult. It was very difficult and I resisted for some time but the evidence seemed to merit it, would seem to require it, for the plotting that went on would have brought treasonous war to us.

Have you been to the Halls of Learning to read accounts?

I have been to the Halls of Learning to read accounts.

Did you find that interesting?

It was interesting, but it was interesting because it was a study in human emotions and entanglements and in difficulties. This was the interesting thing about it. It could have been, at one level, about any two human beings and their associates, making decisions and interacting with each other, for it was written from the point of view of human interactions and motivations and relationships and the difficulties there-in and the learning that may be had from studying this difficulty.

Did it fill in any gaps for you when perhaps you didn't understand why something turned out the way it did?

There was a long pause then Elizabeth answered:

Fear engenders actions, which we may come to regret. (Another long pause) Fear engenders actions we may come to regret and where there is fear there is not love. Fear forces love out and our actions are based upon this fear rather than the love, which they should be based upon. And so if you ask me would I have regrets or would I do something different, the difference would be that I would learn that I have to take chances, to put aside my fears, in order to allow the love to manifest—to base actions upon this love with a brave heart.

And I would give you this, for it is the human condition to fear and it is the human condition sometimes to base choices and actions upon this fear. But we have a need to be brave and to have faith and we have need to base our actions upon love of our fellows and not rationalise them because of fears.

The decisions of a monarch are often based upon fear of preventing what might be happening and what might be—might never be—but the action is taken because it is based on the fear of what might be.

Eileen referred to the problems in Iraq and the fears that have restarted talk of war. (Pre: 2003) Elizabeth answered:

They will make no end of this, this way. They must look to the root, to the ground from which the weeds spring up and remedy the conditions of the ground.

Do you ever consider visiting the various democracies and to influence them?

We all try to reach in different ways as best we may but your situation here is unusual, it is not common. There is not the opportunity to speak to people in the way I am speaking to you but we try to reach people in the best manner we can.

Have you met Diana?

We have met: The beautiful one.

Is she happy now in the spirit world?

She is happy. She is at peace. Her soul was not built for the limelight and the politics of the limelight.

There are some on the earth plane who say she manipulated such situations?

Be that as it may, but when we are put in a situation of survival, we have to survive. We may surprise people with our resourcefulness and the skills we develop for the purpose.

Would you ever consider coming back to earth as a monarch again?

No. I could not endure being a "pretend" monarch. (This was the third time Elizabeth had referred to "pretend monarch" and her comment brought about much laughter from the group)

What about a prime minister then?

I could not endure being a prime minister either.

Do you continue with some form of education in the spirit world?

I told you. I studied and I study in great measure and this is sufficient, along with my discourses with the learned and the wise.

We have heard from others in the spirit world that there are those who come around and ensure that you learn that which is necessary.

Elizabeth smiled and replied:

You are pointed gently in the right direction and not so gently if you don't take the hint the first time. (Laughter)

Are other spirits aware of your identity when on earth?

Yes they can see it in my aura.

Eileen commented that the aura must show a lot of information. Elizabeth responded:

That does not cut any ice with them.

So are you transparent in that you cannot hide anything from other spirits?

There are some things, which are obvious and others not so obvious.

Is there anybody you would not talk to in the spirit world?

I would talk to anyone. I was a great talker when on the earth plane and I have not lost the habit yet. I would talk to anyone who will talk to me for there is much to be learned from people by talking to them—much to be learned about them and about yourself also.

When people talk to you about the monarchy, is it your period of monarchy they talk about?

Elizabeth didn't answer the question straight away. Instead she replied:

I have a little ship in a glass dome like yours—Walter's ship—but I make an aside, please continue.

I was wandering what was the most common question people asked you in the spirit land about your past.

What was the highest moment of my reign, my life? It had to be the repulse of the Armada.

Eileen said it was time to finish. Elizabeth seemed quite amused by this and replied:

Very well then, I will end this audience and I wish you well in all your endeavours. Be brave hearts.

*   *   *

July 22nd 2003

Elizabeth's second visit came at a time when some circle members were experiencing difficulty with the leader of a group they were involved in. The problem had been going on for some time and was about to reach "a head." Other spirits had offered advice but the problem had continued. Elizabeth's opening words were:

I have come. I have come to speak to you again: Elizabeth. I have come to you again, uninvited, yet I have come.

We finished with the pleasantries and Eileen informed Elizabeth that a particular member of the group, who'd been absent on Elizabeth's last visit, had been hoping that she would come through again. The person concerned then added that she was now tongue-tied. Elizabeth answered with amusement:

There is no need to be tongue-tied for I have given up my old ways. I am now of a more charitable inclination.

Jane explained that a newspaper had been running a story on her life and she explained that she'd had questions to ask resulting from the article. Elizabeth asked:

And have you a question in mind?
No. I can't think of one now.

To give Jane time to remember her questions, Eileen asked:

What have you been doing since we last spoke, Elizabeth?
I have not come to speak to you about what I have been doing; I
have come to speak to you about what *you* plan to do with *your* "King."
(referring to the person who was causing the difficulty)

Another circle member decided to get the ball rolling and replied:
Fire away then.

This amused Elizabeth and she responded:
I have not fired any broadsides, either myself or on my behalf, for
many a year (she laughs again) so you must prompt me with your
question.

Jane had remembered some of her questions and asked:
*When you went into the spirit world, were you pleased with what you'd
achieved on earth?*
Yes, I was, overall, very pleased with what I had achieved for it was
a difficult task for a young girl, but I managed it in the end. I had to be
strong and resolute. You see I am giving you guidance already, for I had
to be strong and resolute and my task, my friends, was a hundredfold
more difficult than yours, for all around me were resolute yet I had to be
more resolute. So I had your problem (referring to the problem above) in
reverse, you see, for there were others who would try to influence me to
their own benefit, whereas I was the voice of reason on more occasions
than one and yet I had to stand my ground as Queen, which was no easy
task. So, my friends, it is an easy matter for you to stand your ground
together, jointly; so wherein lies your problem my friends?
*I think we're not being firm enough really. We accept petty rules when we
shouldn't.*
Petty rules serve no nation or realm. Rules should be there to serve
the nation, to serve the commonwealth. If they do not serve the
commonwealth then they should be got rid of, extinguished.

Eileen confirmed that, when Elizabeth used the word extinguished, she was talking about **rules.** Elizabeth smiled and answered:

Yes we are talking about the rules. I have not used the axe for a long time.

Do you think there is much hope for change in our situation?

You must do what you must do and trust in what may come. You will be helped and have faith. If you do not have faith then you will accomplish nothing in life. I have found this, that you must have faith and hope and perseverance. If you have these things then you will flourish. If you preoccupy yourself with the "ifs," the "wherebys," "the wherefores," "the what might be's," and so on, you build ever-increasing lengths of chain about you and you accomplish nothing.

Did you feel that spirit was with you when you were a child, or did you have no knowledge of spirit then?

My spirit was with me. *My* spirit was with me. It felt indeed that I had no help, that indeed *my* own spirit saw me through, and in truth it did. But this perhaps, drove me to an over reliance on my own resources, an isolation which was unfortunate, which paled life. I can find no expression to convey it but do you follow me if I say it paled life? It took the zest out of life, but no matter, that is another time. But we must all be hopeful in this, this and in other matters. We must be hopeful, we must be optimistic, and we must look forward to accomplishment. You are on the horizon of accomplishment and should not be daunted by the task.

Is it better to walk into it and try and change things or say it's not for me and walk away and leave them to get on with the disagreements between each other?

You must forward your view, your counsel, and hold fast to it. You must give good reasons for it and give spiritual reasons for it and loving reasons for it; then who can gainsay you, who can argue with such reasons. It is then down to the largeness of their heart.

It feels like we would be walking into a lion's den, almost.

Yet David preserved himself in the lion's den, he persevered, endured, accomplished what he must. This is what you must do. You must be regal and speak with authority, but with the authority of wisdom and love. Wisdom and love must come through. Who can argue with wisdom and love in the long run?

Elizabeth laughed and continued:

Well I have detained you enough so I shall end the audience now.

Elizabeth had finished giving her advice, which was what she'd come for, but Eileen, and the group, hadn't finished with her. Eileen asked if she was aware that her earlier communication, along with Mary's, was in the book. Elizabeth smiled and answered:

Ah yes, ah yes, I know this and we are most pleased.
Have you met Mary again since we last spoke?
Yes we have met our cousin. There is more contentment between us.
Is Diana settled now?
My cousin: yes.

Eileen queried Elizabeth on the use of the word cousin. She replied:

No, I only use it as a term of endearment.

Another member of the group decided to keep Elizabeth a little longer and asked:
Will you come to earth again?
No, not for some time, if I must, I must, but not for some time, no.

Jane had thought of another question and was keen to ask it before Elizabeth left:
Are you with loved ones now?
Yes, we are with loved ones. We are with loved ones and we are joyous.
Do you have any links now with the present monarchy?
No, only to look on and to mourn their condition; I would not have wished to have endured it.
Is there a group of souls who deal with the monarchy or is it different each time around?
The group of souls, which you speak of; there are those who become monarchs but there are no groups of them, as such. There are those who wish to become monarchs for the experience, for the learning, which it will bring, for the conditions, which it generates on

the earth plane while they do live. There are no souls *called* to it. Is this what you mean? One soul is much as another.

I've read books that suggest that people may incarnate into the same family so they can give back what they've received.

This may happen on occasion but there is no link, no generation link with the monarchy. The monarchy will have had its day before too long.

Not in our lifetime, I take it?

No, but before too long. But it is the *spirit* of your government, which is important of course, rather than the forms of it. For you can have all manner of forms but if their spirit is not right within it, it will not serve you well.

Someone else mentioned the difficulties now faced by the government following the occupation of Iraq. Elizabeth responded:

War is seldom wise for it creates other conditions, which must then be dealt with.

Elizabeth suddenly went off on a different tack; something she'd done on her first visit. She said:

Walter (Raleigh) was here the other day. The other day being a mere expression, you understand.

Do you see Robert Dudley (one of Elizabeth's romantic attachments when on the earth plane) in the spirit world?

Elizabeth seemed to think for a moment then simply smiled. Another circle member responded:

Are you not saying anything further on that, Elizabeth?

A young girl's fancy.

Well, my friends, I must leave you. I have used your time up so I must leave you. Hold the flag steady in its ground for it is a flag of spiritual wisdom. So you must go forward with the flag of spiritual wisdom as my soldiers used to go forward with the flag of England. Alas I cannot pay you.

*   *   *

Many questions have been asked about the role of royalty both in our history and in the future: It seemed appropriate to include some of them here.

Hai was asked:
Would they have chosen to be born here as a king or queen?
Often they have chosen, indeed. But when we choose something, we are not always fully aware of the whole consequences. Having chosen to live as a king or a queen, we go through experiences of being a king or a queen and our mind becomes conditioned to that way of life; expects what kings and queens expect. And it is not always easy to put down these expectations, even when our conditions have moved on. Even when we have been prepared for the experience and prepared for the problem of relinquishing these things, it is not easy necessarily because we have had the experience then. And it is one thing to think of an experience; it is another to live through it, and to live through the consequences of it.

Why would someone choose to be a king or queen?
Many reasons: To play the role, to play the role in a benevolent way; there have been many who abused the role down the ages. The great emperors of Japan played such roles. Some of these emperors were wise and benevolent to their subjects and played out the role well. But, as with other countries, many did not play the role in a benevolent way, but lorded it over the people, their subjects, and failed to look to the needs of their subjects.

So, overall, the time for such roles is drawing to a close. People must work together to develop other forms of government more suited to the times, more suited to the people's needs. This is never easy of course, because governments, of whatever kind, are constituted by human beings and human beings have their strengths and their weaknesses. And those who are attracted to government are a mixed bunch. They have good points and bad points. Some seek it for power. Some seek it for benevolence, to try and help others. So there is a mixture of people. And where you have a mixture of people consequences will also be mixed. The fruit will also be mixed, some good, some bad.

On another night Hai was asked:

How do people from royalty adjust to the spirit world? Presumably it must be quite different to them?

They adjust with difficulty sometimes. It depends on the individual. Some adjust to it well enough. If they had no illusions about their own worth, they had no illusions about the reality of things. So it is not such a big surprise to them when they go to the spirit world and they find they don't have the luxuries, the status, which they had on the earth plane. Others, of course, find it difficult, because they have got so used to being treated in a certain way; being looked up to, having their status that they have had, being obeyed and so on. Therefore they will find it more difficult because they have to relinquish these things. They have to do so, because on the spirit plane all souls are souls. They are one. They have no greater value than the next one. We can have wise souls. We can have teachers. We can have those who help to point the way. But in terms of their own worth there is no difference. And learning this lesson is not always easy. It is not easy on the earth plane. It is no easier on the spirit plane.

*   *   *

Ted

On the same theme of Royalty, one night one of our Guest Speakers, Ted, also had something to say. He told us he was a soldier and had fought in the Crimean war. We asked him about Queen Victoria:

You would have been around in Queen Victoria's day. Was she reunited with Albert in the spirit land?

Ted laughed and replied:
Oh yes. There was no holding that one back.
She really loved him a lot did she?
Yes but there was an intensity to this.
Are they still influential in the spirit world, as they were on the earth plane?
Well you know, whatever we have on the earth plane, including status or position, we do not keep when we move into these spirit lands.

We must adjust to our primal condition, which is simply that we are spirits walking among other spirits, equal under the sun, though there is no sun of course, but you take my meaning. There are some who would like to re-write that rule of course but that avails them not. If they tried to re-write *that* rule they would find themselves in less pleasant quarters.

Did Victoria find it difficult to adjust, Ted?

No she did not find it too difficult though there have been many who have.

Have you come across her in the spirit world?

I have indeed come across her and she is a delightful soul.

Did you meet her on the earth plane as well?

I met her from a distance, so to speak. I was present in her company and indeed was introduced to her, but I would not say we were bosom pals. In fact when she was on the earth "bosom pals" was hardly a term you could use with her. But yes she is a kindly soul.

Is there any special significance to the Royal family in Britain as they come down the ages; for instance, are they the same souls?

Ted laughs and replies:

"Come down the ages"—and yes, hasn't it come down the ages, "down" being the operative word. But you ask about connections sir. These connections are by and large karmic, but accidental. If you go back in time and look at the origins of your Royalty, is it not more a matter of who had the biggest club and who could wield it most effectively? And so you have the origins and the starting point of your Royal family. Do I shock you good enlightened folk then?

That's why some feel it is unfair now.

I know, yet some needed a figurehead down the ages. Your times for figureheads, perhaps, are drawing to a close, though you still have some amongst you in your societies who seek figureheads. You will find change coming about, but would you wish yourself in the role of these people.

This brought about some discussion amongst the circle members about what they view as royal privileges. Ted responded:

Yes, privilege has always gone with it, but you have others who have privilege in your society where such privilege is equally not earned.

I have often thought that the Royals were a group of people who had work to do and have incarnated constantly into a Royal line.

I fear you do not find many of wisdom, or energy come to that, within your Royal families down the ages. They are simply ordinary souls who, at their best, try and do an extraordinary job in difficult circumstances. At their worst they indulge their worst passions, but whether they are wise or not perhaps depends upon the luck of the draw. Sometimes some years you are lucky other years you are not and you pay the price of your bad luck.

Is it that random? Is it not planned at all?

It is indeed that random; it is not planned. It may be, that those who seek the position of responsibility and authority may well find themselves occupying that position of power and responsibility, but there is no merit in it. It is not won by merit.

Chapter 14

Carol & Lopaz

Carol and Lopaz are both original members of the Phoenix Group. However, apart from coming through to talk to Eileen in the very early days when she sat alone with Paul, they both stayed in the background, leaving the other members of the group to direct proceedings. The following communication was only the second time Carol had talked to our friends in the Home Circle. For the benefit of a new circle member Carol started by telling us a little about herself. She also talked about some of her previous lives.

Although Carol and Lopaz were not strictly Guest Speakers, we feel it is appropriate to include them here.

Carol

She told us:

> I was born in Roman times during the first century.
> *Did you live with a well-to-do family?*
> I was a member of a well-to-do family. "Well-to-do"—what a funny expression, "well-to-do."
> *Would you have been alive during Caesar times?*
> No Caesar was long gone when I was around.
> *Was Hadrian around then?*
> Hadrian was a little bit further on than me.
> *What sort of things did you do in your life?*
> I was the daughter of a Senate, of a rich Senate. So I was spoilt, I suppose for I did not have to earn my crust.
> *Did you live in a house, which had an inner courtyard?*

Yes, we had a town house and another on an estate in the country. We lived in Rome some of the time and on our estate the rest of the time. We had a good life but we were fortunate.

What do you do in the spirit world now, Carol?

We work with Hai.

Have you always done that?

Not always but of late I have.

Hai seems to have a wide selection of people working with him.

Yes, why not? He is a powerful magnet, but we have partly come together because of our associations and affinity. I knew of Paul in Roman times when he was of another name.

There followed some personal information about those times and then Carol was asked:

Are you fairly highly evolved?

I would not say so.

Do you live within the Roman situation in the spirit world now?

Carol was clearly amused and replied:

What *is* the Roman situation in the spirit world?

Well, do you live in an area that looks like the Roman times?

I live certainly on the periphery of the hubbub. I like to be near some activity.

Did you like gardens in the Roman times?

Oh yes, I liked the garden. It was beautiful on our villa, on the estate where we could grow more. We were limited, as you would expect in the town. There was not much space even in our big house.

What did you do in the spirit world before you met Hai, Carol?

I learnt, I studied; I grew in my learning and development.

So are you a fan of the Halls of Learning?

I certainly went through the Halls of Learning along with other ways—a useful resource for those who have the patience to study.

Did someone come to you to teach and show you things?

We learn from each other in our group. We learn, we develop we grow. We bring our different skills, abilities and support each other and learn from each other's specialties. I also like to grow plants or, create them, perhaps is the better expression, flowers, beautiful flowers.

Do you create your garden in your own style or in the Roman style you used to know?

I am flexible. I have experimented with many other styles now. I do not attach myself too rigidly to those times, though I have fond memories of them but regrets also for the harm that was done to people, to others. So I have fond memories of those times but I do not shackle them to me like some millstone.

One group member commented on how much we are still influenced by Rome today. Carol responded:

Well, it was far-reaching in its day, wasn't it, and so its influence has been far-reaching across the lands of the earth and into the time of the future. But it is the same, is it not, with all things, though some of our actions are not as obvious in their consequences, their effects in their influences. Your example of Rome is an example. We recognise the influence more strongly because the power and the influence of its day, which has continued and carried forth through the ages and across the lands where it prevailed. But you would be well to think that you also have an influence in your individual lives. Your influences carry forward across time in ways that you may barely perceive or be aware of. Your Empire prevails; your influence prevails in its own way. Be sure; be certain that the influence, which you create, which will prevail, will be loving and positive. You understand my analogy.

A circle member referred to the influence a simple window box full of flowers might have on someone. Carol replied:

Yes, to the passer by it might lighten their day, lighten, and gladden their soul. The simple things can be marvellous things, marvellously uplifting, and marvellous food for the soul.

Are you a bit of a philosopher on the quiet, Carol?

It goes with the territory. Who could mix with our group (Phoenix) and not become a philosopher. I was attracted to the group partly because of that learning that may be accrued through such interaction and dialogue and such companionship of working together.

Why is it that you don't come to talk to us very often? You don't seem shy to me?

Well, you have not sought me and I have not pushed myself. Many have wished to talk and I am content to do my bit from the background scene.

Have you been back to earth since the Roman times, Carol?

No, I have not been back since those times.

Have you not had the inclination to come back?

I have found purpose where I am and so, at the moment, I do not see the need to come back.

Eileen reminded Carol of when she had talked to her about some of her previous lives on the earth plane.

Do you remember some of your other lives, Carol? Remember we talked about them.

I did have other lives. I think I was less fortunate in one of them. I had to till the land or help to till the land, which was a much harsher life, a much less fortunate state of affairs. But it has its own merits. It has its own potential for development, for growth of spirit. We should cherish each life we have for the gift it gives us which may have its own special gift to render to us.

What part do you play now in the Phoenix Group, Carol?

I create; I provide creativity and the beauty of creativity.

Do you continue with your studies?

We can never end our studies, can we, for there is always something to study. There is always something to grow in so we can never say that we will reach the end of our studies. Would it not be boring, would it not be monotonous if we knew everything and we could say, we have reached the end of our studies, we know everything? There is an un-fathomless part of wisdom and knowledge, of creation, of creativity, which we may explore and discover.

When people are born onto the earth plane, is justice sewn into the soul? Does it exist in the soul? I mean that which is morally or ethically wrong?

If you mean do we know what is right and what is wrong, then I would say yes, if we can but turn within to our centre and recognise what is there and recognise the nature of ourselves and the nature of right and wrong. We all have the ability to know right and wrong, to know it in great measure, if we seriously wish to know. But there are many, are there not, who do not wish to know, not really.

I wondered what made people turn against right?

Because they do not look, they do not search. They do not delve into the depths of their innermost self. They avoid the work, they pursue what they think is in their best interests, their self-interests and do not look, for they do not wish the contrary. They do not wish that which they see to be against their self-interest. Though truly what is in the interests of ourselves and what is in the interests of others is one and the same.

*   *   *

Carol ended the session with her own spirit blessing.

I would say I am most pleased to have spoken with you. I have enjoyed our company together, our time together and we may do so again but in the meantime I would wish you a good night's sleep and the peace of certain slumber to awake refreshed in the land of tomorrow; that you may make your mark upon the day to the fulfilment of yourselves and to the great joy of your hearts and the hearts of others. Goodbye to you.

*   *   *

Lopaz

Lopaz was the first spirit to contact and work with us before introducing us to Hai. He explained that his last incarnation was not on earth but on some other planet in another galaxy. We realised later, after he had introduced us to Hai, that his job had been simply to prepare us for Hai's contact. In fact Lopaz could even be described as a spirit "scout."

On this occasion Davia, our gatekeeper, had arranged a special Guest Speaker night. Lopaz's visit came at the end of the evening and he talked to us about future communication on our earth. Davia described him later, in his humorous way, as "topping the bill."

Lopaz began the communication by telling us:

I am most pleased to see you all tonight. We have come through because it is something of an anniversary or celebration that we have been able to reach this point with this medium so we have come through to converse with you to celebrate this point.

Eileen explained to new circle members that Lopaz had been the "leader" in the initial contact with the spirit group. Lopaz continued:

We were indeed, with others, but we spoke to you first through your communication board but I travelled to see Hai to ask if he would be kind enough to accept the invitation to work with you and your group. And he was kind enough to embrace the possibility.

Lopaz was introduced to the other members of the group. There was some joviality and reference was made to Davia (spirit gatekeeper/stage manager) who had recently talked about Lopaz. Someone commented:

He says you are best buddies.
That is Davia with his jokes.

A member of our group asked:
Did you send a picture (clairvoyantly) to me of your space ship?
We have conversed mentally with you and with others to attempt to convey some communication, which will be of some significance. Your times will change ultimately and your powers of mental communication, even while in the physical will grow. This is humanity.

Someone commented that they would look forward to it. Lopaz responded:

Whether you will look forward to it or not is another matter. Whether you *should* look forward to it or not is another matter. But nevertheless it is a faculty that will grow and which you will have to rise to the challenge to meet, for it will bring in its wake many challenges, many complications and confusions until you are able to harness it for your own good and benefit. For you know yourselves that it has not always been the way of your ancestors that they have channelled such things for your good benefit. But we are all on our journey to learn and in learning we must sometimes endure pain in order to progress and it is as true of this as it is of other things. We, on our planet, also had to endure our mistakes, had to endure our misfortunes and endure through them to move forward, to progress to a better state of affairs.

Are you a very serious person, Lopaz?

I am a calm person I would say rather than serious—a very calm person, a very tranquil person.

Is this typical of your race?

It is typical of the general temperament of my race, of our species but with our species there are variations, as you have many variations within your human kind. There is always variety in creation because creation by its very nature breeds variety and individuality. In the smallest microbe you will find individuality. There is nothing, which is identical to anything else even with your identical twins. Nothing is identical.

In your society, is life similar to ours, in that you get married, have children, set up home?

You would find some similarities but you find many differences between your life, your world, and ours.

Do you go out to work; have jobs, all that sort of thing? Do you have localised transport?

We have versatile transport, more versatile than yours, more adaptable than yours for we can use it to travel on the surface of the planet and into the outer atmosphere.

Is there a male and female species?

We have male and female but the distinction is less than yours.

Are you physical in the way we are physical?

We are physical in the sense that you would recognise us as having a humanoid appearance and form but we would appear different to you for we do not have your facial appearance.

But are you physical beings as apposed to beings of light?

We are physical beings in a physical universe.

But much more advanced than our world?

Much more advanced, by what criteria do you apply?

Technology.

By the criteria to technology, we are much more advanced.

Are there any areas where you are less advanced than us?

Yes, in the feeling of the heart. In the matters of the heart we are not as advanced. It is not that we have not advanced but we have not achieved the degree of progress, which we have achieved with our inventions and our technologies, which we should have achieved in parallel, in the matters of the heart; we have not because we have not had the wisdom to advance to this degree, as we should within these matters of the heart.

*   *   *

Lopaz was our last visitor that night, and as is customary, he finished the evening with a blessing. He is usually quite serious in his conversations with us; however, on this particular occasion when giving his blessing, he also gave us a glimpse of his humour.

Lopaz's Blessing

It falls to me to wish you a happy conclusion to your evening. I wish you a good cup of tea. I wish you, my friends, great wisdom. I wish you great wisdom to use your earthly lives wisely. To gain from them great compassion and wisdom and understanding that you may advance spiritually to great heights, to heights beyond the reach of my flying machine and, with that, I must leave you for the man with the paddle is urging me on. (Another humorous reference to our gatekeeper and master of ceremonies, Davia.)

I would leave you with these wishes and wish you a goodbye.

*   *   *

On another visit Lopaz tells us a little about the circumstances on his home planet and what his job is now in the spirit world. We started the communication as usual with the usual pleasantries and asked whether he was well as we hadn't spoken to him for some time. He replied:

I am most well, thank you; we and our kind are most well.

Do you go on travels, then?

Ah we do. I go to the place, the spirit land where my kind dwells who lived on the planet that I lived upon when I was in a physical incarnation.

Do you communicate with them?

We can link with direct mind; with more permitted means also if we wish.

Is this an accepted part of life?

Yes, we may communicate directly with each other, which means that we can have a more clear expression of our communication a more direct way of communication whereby we may truly enter each other's mind's centre; communicate directly our thoughts and intent. We may truly know each other's minds by this means.

Do the people on your planet know of an existence after death?

They know that there is continued existence but it is as with you, they do not know the form it takes, they do not know precisely the form that it takes but they do know of its existence and are more assured in their knowledge than you are, or your kind.

Can you communicate in a direct way?

We can communicate with them indeed and this is why they have greater assurance because the communication is of a more precise nature. And yet we cannot still convey to them pictures or images of the spirit lands and therefore, they rely upon our communication. Communication in this case is not precise.

Are there many other planets like yours, which are inhabited?

Many planets are inhabited—many planets throughout the universes.

Someone asked him to confirm he said universes "plural." He replied:

Universes, yes, for there are dimensions beyond yours.

Can many other people from your planet travel the different realms?

No, it is not easy and it is not automatic. It must be learned; it must be earned to a point. The vibration of the different realms must be attuned to, must be made to be at one with; that we may travel without hindrance across the realms.

If someone from earth and your planet were of similar evolution, would they be able to travel the realms like you?

Spirit is spirit in the final analysis; spirit is spirit and therefore when spirits evolve and are in the spirit lands then it is a matter of evolvement, of development as to whether they can travel the realms.

Is the One Mind central to all these dimensions?

All are resting within the One Mind. The One Mind embraces all.

How did you become involved with Hai?

I have intent, an interest, a mission indeed, to link, to reach out to the physical worlds. We connect the physical worlds with the spiritual worlds. This is my mission, as it is the mission of others. I seek and I make contact and I seek out those who may best connect with those on the earthly planes, who are desirous of making contact with those in spirit. We find those in spirit who are best placed to make connection with those on the physical.

When you were in your physical body, did you have any knowledge of worlds beyond your own?

Yes, we have knowledge of worlds beyond our own. We visited worlds beyond our own.

Were there different life forms to you on these planets?

They were different and similar to us in some cases. They varied.

Did you form links with these?

We did form links with them. Some links were stronger than others.

Were these mainly friendly types of species?

They were mainly friendly. (Smiles) Those who did not appear to be so friendly we stayed clear of.

Is there an intermingling of people from different planets in the spirit world?

There can be an intermingling, but it is natural that those who go into the spirit worlds are brought together with those whom they are familiar with, with those who they have shared heritage with; therefore, they are drawn together, as is the case with you on your earthly journey on your earthly plane. But just as with your earthly journey on your earthly plane, it is possible for the boundaries and barriers to be put aside and for those of different realms to meet together but it is a matter of intent, of desirous nature that this should happen.

Is your job, then, to find people on the physical planes, which desire to make contact with the spirit world?

I seek to bring down barriers. I seek to make connections across barriers by whatever means I can, whether these barriers be barriers between the physical and spiritual realm or indeed, between the spiritual realms themselves. I am desirous of bringing down the barriers and making connections and striding across the barriers, for barriers are indeed truly there to be overcome, to be transcended. This is the inherent nature of the One Mind.

Is your planet greatly advanced to our world?

It is greatly advanced in its scientific application, in its technological ability but I believe I have said before it is not advanced in its spiritual nature. It is not that it is not advanced at all but it is not advanced to the same degree, as we would expect given advances in the sciences and the technological realm.

Is the day-to-day living of your people more advanced than ours?

It is more advanced in that it is dependent upon our technology— but our technology is so advanced that life is secure because of it. But it is secure and yet it is dependant on it also and we may think of this in two ways. At one level, we may think of it as truly advancement and progress that we have been able to progress to this degree, to this stage. But at another level in a different interpretation, we may speak of this as being dependence and as such a dependency is a weakness, is it not, because if that which you depend upon should fail, then you are undone.

What about the moral consciousness of your race?

It is ordered in extreme measure. The society is ordered to great measure and in being ordered to great measure it means the opportunity for transgression is slight. But this does not solve the problem or the issue. For being ordered, being controlled is not the same as being of good and pure heart. If we control each other, if we control things, if we control circumstances, what merit is it if we are in accord with our relationships with our brother and sister? If we are controlled to the nth degree in our relationships with each other, what merit is there in these relationships being ordered? (Order is imposed upon us.)

You mean you can't flourish, so to speak, in a natural way?

It is rather that there is not the test of the natural.

How can these other dimensions exist? Are they that far away from us?

They are not far away; there are other dimensions. There are parts of this physical universe, which you would truly say were far away from you and yet by another measure they are just around the bend. Yet there are dimensions, which *are* far away from you, but this is not distance.

Do you still have your space ship?

I do, I have my replica—my working replica.

Is there a sort of order, a song of the universe? (This question was asked in reference to Lopaz's travelling)

There is, wherever you go in the universe, a signature. The signature is of the One Mind—Is the One Mind. There is a signature wherever you go, a Nowness, an Isness, a Suchness, which transcends the appearance of difference, of duality.

Eileen said it was time to finish. Lopaz replied:

It is time in your time to end our time together. We are happy also to have made contact with you again. And though we do not make contact with you often these days, be assured, be knowing that we are ever watchful and with you.

I sometimes think of you and wonder if we register with you.

All is registered, for thought travels light, light through the universe. If you look to the star at night you will see its light. Goodbye, my friends.

*   *   *

Shortly Lopaz'a visit a member of our Home Circle commented to Hai:

It was nice talking to Lopaz again, Hai.

Oh yes, oh yes, he was very pleased to talk to you also, for it had been some time since you last spoke with him.

Lopaz said his people were evolved through science but not with the heart. I was surprised. I thought that it would follow that an evolved race would be more compassionate and caring. Also you've told us that we come to earth to learn control so what is the point of being incarnated onto a planet where it will be so controlling that you cannot make mistakes and learn from them?

Well—but everything, every experience has its own lessons, has its own direction, which it will shape us in; lead us, in that we may learn from these experiences. And so even if living in an orderly society, where we have little choice, little ability to reflect upon our choices and choose of our own volition; this is also a lesson to learn. For we know then, we realise then, that there is no merit in this; this doing good through control. It is rather when we do "good" from our own free will, from our own choice, our own decision that we should speak of merit. And what is the use of pretence if our hearts are not loving; yet we put on a pretence of love to abide by the order; then this is no use.

We must be in a position to allow our loving hearts freedom, to do as they will but hopefully we choose to do what is loving, what is truthful, what is helpful and constructive for our fellows. There is no love if someone gives you a rulebook and you say to them; "Ah, you turn to page thirty and you follow the rules on page thirty in this situation. And you go to another situation and they tell you to follow the rules to page twenty-five in this situation," and so on. You could run out of rules as well, which could make it difficult for you, but if you have the principle of love in your heart then you know how to apply it; you know how to behave in all situations.

So did they become so evolved that they went beyond the love, then?

They ruled by order and if you turn your society around on a pivot, focal point of order, this becomes the motivator; this becomes the focus rather than love. We all need order of some degree, of some kind in order for us to live in society but if the order becomes the prime mover rather than love, then we have lost the plot, as they say, lost the plot.

Chapter 15

Saint Rosalind

The following communication with Saint Rosalind is another example of how we attract spirits to us when we show an interest in them. One summer Eileen and I visited a small church in France that had a particular association with the Saint Rosalind. In fact her preserved body is kept inside the church on display. We could see by the pictures around the walls that Rosalind had been accepted as some kind of healer and, Eileen, because of her interest in healing, was naturally drawn to her.

Eileen took the first opportunity following this visit to ask Hai about Rosalind. Hai said a few words and left. Immediately afterwards, Rosalind came through. A short extract of the conversation is included here. We feel that the communication is interesting and worth sharing with others. Not only is it interesting in its own right, but Eileen also believes that it had a strong impact upon her. She feels she was offered a new way of viewing people who choose to give up part of their life to live in a monastery or convent and to that extent Rosalind has had a fairly major impact upon her view of life.

Rosalind began the communication by commenting:

> You showed interest in me, my child.
> *Are you Rosalind?*
> I am indeed whom you say.
> *I was very curious when I saw your preserved body in the church.*
> We noticed this.
> *Did you heal people when on earth?*

I wished them well and sometimes their ailment was improved. I was only the channel.

From reading the information I obtained from the church, it would seem that you had a hard life.

You are correct. It was a hard life but a simple life, which therefore had its benefits. A simple life has many benefits for those who can pursue it, yet even in a simple life there are those who create complications of the world.

It said in the leaflet that you gave a lot of your food away when you were in the convent.

Yes we did, we did give much away, for we were concerned about the poor and the hungry of our parish.

I suppose you know that when they exhumed your body five years later, you were completely intact; your body had not started to decay.

The decay was not what was normally expected.

Is that how they decide people are saints?

It is one of the factors.

The drawing I bought of you in the church; is that a copy of a picture that was done while you were on the earth plane?

An impression of what they thought I looked like when I was alive, for even though the body was preserved to a point, you can only gain an impression of the likeness.

Is the picture a good likeness?

It is of some likeness.

What do you think of them having the remains of your body on display, Rosalind?

It is not a pretty sight, is it?

I wouldn't say that. It is a bit of a shock when you first see it but it draws people's attention to what you did on earth.

There were leaflets in the church about miracles said to have occurred around Rosalind. Eileen commented on the leaflets and continued:

I understand someone who wanted to say thank you, restored the chapel. (Rosalind gave the name of the person, which unfortunately was lost in the transcript)

I take it you are happy in your present life.

This is true; this is true.

Do you think it's a good idea for people to enter monasteries in this day and age?

You are not of the opinion that it is good?

I'm coming to accept that for some people, it might be the right thing to do.

There is a path to be trod for some; there is a path to be taken. For some can provide an example to others to reflect upon, to question their own values, to question their own preoccupations, to question their priorities. This example may provide a purpose, a useful purpose therefore, in this. For if we pursue our life and take its values for granted, when we confront altogether different values, which provide a basis for a different life style altogether, it provides a useful contrast for us to question our own values and our own existence, our own lifestyle. Or do you not see that this perhaps may be the case?

I'm beginning to see. I understand now that monks would see themselves as providing a "power bank" for the community, sending up prayers, and healing.

They were indeed such.

I can see why they would do that and we do all have more than one life.

A drop in the ocean (one life.)

I can see that now.

You have struck a chord, my dear; you do well to question your opinion, it is not easy.

Although I've accepted reincarnation for many years, I have still thought of a life in a monastery or convent as being a wasted one.

There are many in the world who waste their lives. The wasting of life, or not, is not a matter for easy calculation. A very busy life may seem a wasted life. A very quiet life may seem a wasted life, yet it depends on many things. It depends on the learning, which the soul acquires through living that life.

Do you think you would ever return to a life like that again?

There is no need.

Eileen had noticed some dead flowers in the church where Rosalind lay. She commented on this:

I hope they've replaced the dead flowers in the church.

Rosalind's reply was interesting. She said:

The beauty of your wish is there in any event, whether flowers or not; **the beauty of our wish is the real beauty,** beyond a physical meeting.

What does it mean to be a Saint in the Catholic Church, Rosalind?

It means to be held up as an example of way of living, a way to live. It means to act as intermediary between those who live on the earth and the divine forces of creation.

*   *   *

On another night the circle were talking to Isleen. Eileen was curious and asked about Rosalind.

Does the fact that someone was a very good person, an old soul, stop the body dematerialising at the normal rate?

It would not necessarily affect the body at all sometimes, though to provide a sign to the world, a body may be preserved beyond its normal period of decomposition.

What causes that to happen?

It is caused by the attunement of the spirit with the greater spirit, which also creates a link with the physical body; therefore, the physical body may be preserved beyond its normal cause. It is not indicative itself of a person living a holy life but it may be a sign as such.

It seemed very coincidental that she came through as soon as I asked about her. Paul was worried that his mind had fabricated her.

Yes we know, but we have spoken to you about this and the importance of affinity, of emotional bonds of love and affection. These are the things, which draw us to you so if you form a bond, an emotional tie with someone, then you may draw them to you.

Chapter 16

Ramadahn

We understand that Ramadahn is a wise spirit guide whose communications, through another medium, are well documented. It would seem that his reason for communicating with us on this occasion was simply for us to share each other's company in love.

Ramadahn gave us his name and told us:

I am most happy to be acquainted with you. I am most happy to be in your presence where I feel the radiating love.

Do you have a particular reason for coming tonight?

Do I need a particular reason? For, indeed, it is in the lack of purpose where greatest love may be shown. We do not need purpose, do we, to seek each other's company? We do not need purpose or intent to seek each other's company, to spend time in each other's company, to enjoy each other's company. For in the simple presence of each other, in the simple companionship of each other, all is sufficient, is it not?

You have just talked about being in the company of others, but is there not a time when you need to be by yourself?

This is true, for, in seeking solitude; it provides us with opportunity to seek within, to seek our wisdom within, to grow, to know our inner self, our true self. To uncover the fruit of great love, which may be expressed to our comrades, to our fellows on the earthly journey. So solitude can greatly aid, can greatly facilitate our inner growth, our reaching out to those around us, our embracing of the Eternal Now. But, indeed, even in our solitude we are not alone, for we are joined inextricably with all the universe; with all the universes physical and spiritual. There can be no isolation anywhere. There can be no separation anywhere, for in essence we are of One Heart and One Lifeblood. And the One Heart beats within us all and in feeling the One Lifeblood, the One Heart beating within us all, we know the heartbeat of all and are joined to all. Those who see themselves in isolation who pursue their own interests in isolation, who pursue their own interests as if they are isolated, do themselves great harm and discomfort for they may lose the sense of this Oneness; they may loose the sense of this joined Heart, this Lifeblood, which beats through all of us. It is in recognising this One Heart, recognising the bond, the inner bond, which reaches through us all that we discover our destiny, our identity, and true peace.

One member of the circle, clearly impressed by what Ramadahn had to say, asked:
Are you on a par with the Buddha?

Ramadahn answered:
You are on par with Buddha.
Can you tell us something about your history, Ramadahn?
I am from ancient Egypt. My lifetime was in ancient Egypt.
Were you a king?
I was a king of little wisdom, whose wisdom grew because of the lack of wisdom. For we learn, do we not, through our mistakes. We learn from our reflections if we are wise but I fear there are those who do not learn from their reflections, upon their mistakes, who perpetuate their mistakes endlessly, who repeat their mistakes endlessly. True wisdom looks upon our mistakes, learns from our experiences and grows through these things and slowly but surely stands on the steps of this experience till we climb the mountain and look over the vast horizons below us. Slowly we climb the steps, slowly we climb the mountain peaks, but assuredly one step in front of the other will lead us there if we do not look back.
Can you tell us something about what you do now in the spirit world, Ramadahn?
I teach, I teach on planes physical and spiritual. I enjoy company. I enjoy being with you. I enjoy being with others, for our hearts touch in such moments. Our hearts reflect with the Divine Reality, the Divine Essence as we spend time in each other's company with our hearts

touching. It expresses the Divine Reality more profoundly than do the words that I speak.

Do you travel the realms teaching?

I travel the realms according to need.

*   *   *

Before he left, Ramadahn gave us his blessing:

You must take your rest. So we would leave you and we have been glad to make your acquaintance, having been greatly happy to have spent some time with you and we would wish you on your way with great comfort and peace of mind. We would wish you all your days be of great peace of mind and harmony. We wish this for you until the end of your days, till you rejoin us in the lands of spirit.

Part Three

Chapter 17

Developing Mediumship

The Early Days with Hai & Paul

Since this book was first published, the Phoenix Group have communicated a new book; "Unfolding the Lotus," which is dedicated to the subject of the development of mediumship. Nevertheless, we thought that readers who are, perhaps, struggling to develop mediumship themselves, might find the information in this chapter useful. Below we offer a sample of our experiences during the earlier days of our contact with the Phoenix Group and some of the questions that were asked by Eileen and members of our Home Circle. We begin the chapter with something that Hai said about developing mediumship.

He told us:

Development can take many forms, as you know. The most important thing, as with other things we have often spoken about, is the intent, is the desire to communicate, or to act as a channel for us to speak through you in some form, whether it is through images, or whether through the present form with this medium. You need to reach out to us. You need to use your imaginations, your creativity, to help you to reach out. This, we know is difficult for you, because many on your plane, if you spoke to them about using your imagination to reach out to us, would say: "Well it is just your imagination." Yet it is important to use your creativity, to use your imagination, to ride on your imagination to reach us.

What starts out as your imagination acts as a vehicle for real contact with us in spirit. You need to experiment if you wish to develop, to see which form of attunement, which forms of communication you find easiest. Some see best through images in the mind. Some hear voices in their mind. Others sense the feelings; they get a sense of presence and a sense of message. So it's best to experiment and to respond to those forms of communication, those forms of receiving messages, which give you feedback, which seem to work with you, which seem to blend with you. This is not to say that you cannot develop other forms of communication, but it's best to start with one and develop it and practice it and become skilful with it, consolidating it before moving on to develop other forms.

With Paul, we started first with images, with images which were symbolic and images that conveyed scenes of my life and with the images, in time, we gave words also. We indicated to him and Eileen that we wished to try for a more direct form of communication, a form that you now hear. So we were able to give an indication of the pattern, the direction of development and this he was able to respond to.

It's important to build in qualities of patience, steadfastness, and endurance, because as you know, it is a slow process; nevertheless, it can be developed with perseverance. A steady approach is called for, not worrying too much about fluctuations in your apparent ability, or in the quality of the messages. This is like one of your graphs that you might see where the line goes up and down, but overall it is going upwards. You understand the analogy? So you must not worry too much about short-term fluctuations, because the longer-term pattern is what is important.

*   *   *

On another night Hai was asked:
   Is it true to say we all have a gatekeeper?
   Yes.
   And is that, a spirit energy that stands by us and will only allow a certain vibration close to us?
   Well, this is a difficult matter, Ray, for it's true we all have a gatekeeper, guardian, and friend to watch over us. I prefer the term, "friend guardian helper," but—same difference, yes? But, yes, there is

this person who watches over us, connects with us, who tries to filter for us those influences which will do us harm, which will cause us mischief, yes. But, I would say to you, that the difficulty is that you on your earth plane are in a certain energy field, certain energy system. We on our plane are in another energy system. These energies, systems, intermingle; they interpenetrate with each other and so we are all *one*; we are all *unified*, we are all linked together. But the difficulty is that it's like an intricate web of energy systems and these spirits; these earth-bound spirits or spirits who are on lower planes, their energy systems are denser than ours. They are sometimes closer to your energy system and they can therefore more easily affect the physical, physical system within your world, yes? Therefore, they can, if you like, have a better key that fits the lock; because of their energy they fit the lock better. So they can influence things before we can sometimes get there.

In the long term this is not a problem, not a big issue, for if you reach out with pure heart, pure mind these spirits will lose interest anyway. It's like as if someone who is a frivolous person, who likes to talk of gambling all day, who likes to talk about gossip, this and that and they meet up with a great philosopher. They try to engage this great philosopher for a while but soon they get fed up because the great philosopher has no interest in what they are interested in, and they have no patience, no time for the great philosopher.

This is a bit like with you. If you have a heart of purity, if your intent is pure and high, reaching mischievous spirits will lose patience with you, lose interest in you; become bored with you. So there is no long-term problem in this. For if you reach out to us, you establish a strong bond, a strong connection. And insofar as you reach out to establish this strong bond, strong connection, you improve the vibrational link between you and us, between your world and ours. Therefore, it is easier for us to control other influences. I use this term control, but I do not wish you to think that we are controlling you, you understand, for we work with you in partnership. We do not control for the sake of wanting control. We control those influences, which may surround you, which may wish to influence you for harm and we are better disposed, enabled to do this, if you reach out to us, if you connect with us. But it's **your** power, **your** power. **You** have power to bring about this bond, this connection, for without your reaching out to us we are powerless.

*   *   *

On another occasion Hai answered further questions put to him by the group. One member asked:

People often talk of "working for spirit."
You must think of partnership and not "working for spirit", because it's a partnership of friends. If there were no partnership of friends there would be no phenomena of whatever kind. There is One Reality. We all share this One Reality. We all live in this One Reality. There is no here and there. There is no this and that. There is no spirit plane and earth plane in the final analysis; there is One Reality.

But aren't we doing this for our own development? And aren't you helping us to achieve this?
Ah, yes. But it's just the same as you all coming together here as friends, to be together, to work together, to enjoy your time together. We are more ethereal members of the group, perhaps in your eyes, but we are just other members of the group.

When a person becomes involved with spirit, does it help change their personality for the better?
This, unfortunately, is not necessarily the case. It depends upon the intent of the person, upon their commitment, upon their motivation for contact, their motivation for development. It is like in everything else, is it not? You may hear wise words. You may know of the value of some things, which you hear of, the principles that are spoken but at the end of the day it is your choice, is it not? It is your decision, your free will, as to whether you act upon these words, as to whether you embrace the spirit of these words and make them your own wisdom: It is the same for mediums who seek contact.

*   *   *

Trance

In the early days, Eileen and Paul would often sit alone between circle meetings. The following is a conversation between Eileen and Hai during those sessions. Much of the conversation relates to Paul's personal development; however, we have included it here because we thought it might be useful to others who are considering or developing trance.

Hai told Eileen:

I have worked long and hard, with the others to bring about the possibility of communication. We also, of course, can learn from others who have gone before us in this venture. But we must also practice our skills of communication. We must develop our harmony in our group. We must develop a concerted effort to reach out to those who are ready to receive us in communication. So we have our training, you might say, which is necessary in order for us to make contact with your world. It's not an easy process, either for you or for us, but where there are willing hearts, love and harmony, the two can reach out and fit together, and link in harmony also. This is how things happen. This is how things are achieved. We find people of like mind in the spirit world who wish to join with us in this venture. We must develop an affinity. We must find people who are in affinity with us, with the venture, with the enterprise and then we're able to make good progress. So you see, affinity is as important for us as it is for you. Harmony is as important for us as it is for you; "like mind," "like effort," all are important.

He (Paul) feels safe with Isleen. You know that we used Isleen at first because of her gentle nature. She makes people feel safe with her. This is useful of course, because when spirits first make contact with a human it is natural, it's human in fact, to fear, to wonder what is going on, and to wonder about the intent of the spirits who make contact. Therefore spirits such as Isleen who are gentle souls, soft souls, are very helpful because they convey their aura as one of gentleness and trust and softness. They are helpful in establishing contact and establishing a degree of trust, which we can then build on. And souls will then feel more secure so that "rougher" souls like myself who come along, have a door, an entry, and the trust is already established. So the person is more able to accept the presence and the contact from people such as I who are less refined perhaps, at some level at least.

Note: We think Hai was being modest when he referred to himself as a "rougher" soul because we have been told that he is a very old evolved soul. The rest of the group often refer to him as "old Hai."

Hai continued to explain some of the mechanics of communication and though he acknowledges that the Ouija board was a convenient way for us to get started he nonetheless warns against indiscriminate use:

We are responsive to the intentions that you project from yourselves. Paul projected an intention to make contact with the spirit world and you went along with this. You used the board, the Ouija board, as you call it, to make contact and this is okay for starters. But it has its dangers, as we've tried to make you aware. There are those beings, those souls, who exist, loiter, on the periphery of your world and are also keen to watch out for desired contact. But they of course have different intentions altogether to ours. They are concerned with exerting power and influence; with causing mischief; with causing confusion and unsettling people. Therefore their contact is undesirable. But it serves the purpose, this Ouija board, to establish first contact.

Once contact is established though, it's possible to develop it in other ways and this we've done through imagery, through words planted in the mind and so on, to establish clearer, more direct contact in this way. We've moved on to try for communication in the present way (trance) and this is succeeding well. But we will obviously need to keep developing it to make it stronger, to make it clearer, to be able to come over more fully to you, to convey what we wish. Paul's mind still interferes and creates blocks and barriers and affects the flavour of what we try to say, though this is not to be worried about too much as essential points *are* conveyed. But we are still limited and we must work at trying to overcome these limitations.

When I sang a few moments ago that was another sign that these limitations were dropping away. The tune was unknown to Paul. It was a reminiscence of mine. It didn't come from his mind. He's expressed this hope, this aspiration, that I will be able to relay things at a deeper level, which only I know from my past experiences; my experiences of the spirit world and so on; to relay to you deeper knowledge, deeper understanding, which could not have been known to him; which could only have been known to someone who has had the direct experience themselves of being in the spirit world. This is what we seek to achieve and we will achieve it; have no doubts about it. Your dedication makes this possible.

What he has to do is not easy to explain. But he has to give way to my presence, to my spirit, to enable me to use this body. It's not easy to put it into words and it's a confusing experience for those who live through it.

Hai and Eileen continued with their conversation regarding the mechanics of communication and trance in particular:

Is there a level in meditation that is too deep to contact spirit?
Reaching out to spirit requires the mind to attune itself. It requires a focused activity, a focused energy of mind. If the mind goes too deep, as in deep meditation, it's not in the best disposition to attune to the energy of spirit. It may well attune to the Deeper Mind, which sustains us all. It may well attune to the Bedrock of us all, the One Mind. But it is not in the best disposition to attune to spirit energies and to foster communication.

So are some people more disposed to be able to go deeper than others?
It's a matter of practice. The practice of some people has trained them, to go to certain levels. In practicing thus they have a strength but when it comes to other forms of using their mind it can be an obstruction because training of the mind to attune to one level does not necessarily facilitate attunement at another level. People have to unlearn to a certain extent how they trained their mind in order that they may retrain it to attune at a different level. But this can be done. This can be done.

It's uncomfortable for him (Paul) at times, but it is also uncomfortable for us to go through the adjustment of the spirit body to the point that we can blend to make communication effective. It is difficult. It's a two-way thing, which causes some discomfort for both parties; but necessary if we are to achieve strong communication.

Why do you need my voice to help you communicate, Hai?
We need your voice to help us with the link to the material world. Without your voice it's more difficult. We need the vibration of your voice to connect us at times. Otherwise we are joined to Paul, to his mind, but without stimulation from the physical world it's more difficult for us to join with you, to communicate.

When you first talked through Paul was there anything special that night which made it possible for you?

No. It was merely that the time had come to fruition. We'd been working with you for many, many months and we had been building up an affinity with his body and his mind and his spirit. And it was just a matter of time before this work could reach fruition and bare fruit. It's a matter of planning, affinity, and attunement. And this takes time. He has had to learn to be open to us and this took time also because it's not a natural thing, an automatic thing, to be so open that we can gain entry. Some find it more difficult than others. Some are resistant to such an idea. Paul also has resistances because of his temperament. But he has the stronger desire to make contact, to have communication and so the inhibitions, the obstructions, and hindrances have been thrown aside. But it's an ongoing thing and we will deepen it with time.

*   *   *

One night Eileen went to a demonstration of mediumship. The medium had started the service by offering spirit philosophy. She asked Hai:

Was the philosophy, spirit-inspired?

It was spirit-inspired, but we are limited by the understanding of the medium when we use them for philosophy. It is a blend between our inspiration and their ability to translate or express the message. We can only use the tools, which we are given. This is part of the problem which Paul experiences when trying to work out how much comes from us and how much comes from him. It's a blending and in the way we express ideas through the medium we must make use of their vocabulary and some of their basic ideas they have built up over the years, yet try to retain the essential message which we wish to convey.

This is what confuses Paul: He wonders how much is in his mind and how much is what you say.

It is confusing. We are aware of this and we have sympathy for it, because communication occurs, is possible, through a blending of our minds. So we can't be sure where one mind starts and the other stops and so this is a problem and for the medium, because the boundaries are not clear-cut. But this does not invalidate the proceedings. He is more aware when he gets spirit contact because there's a *sense* of interaction. You may, of course, get interaction in your dreams but I do not refer to this. It's more vivid than that, more real than that.

This process of communication takes place by a blending of our minds. Our minds blend with the medium. And it is difficult because we share each other's thoughts for the time this goes on. There's a transaction, which takes place, and it is possible that we borrow from the medium's thoughts. This doesn't mean that what we say is invalid because we make use of the medium's mind, thoughts, upbringing, background ideas, and beliefs where appropriate. So it's not like we speak directly to you in the way that you speak directly to each other in daily life. It is rather that we speak to you indirectly, through the minds' of the mediums we use. This is not to say that we are distant in this communication for we are active participants. But it's as if we are on the other side of a foam wall and we press in the foam and create an impression and you will see the impression on the other side but you cannot see our fingerprints. You can't see the fingerprints that we use to make the pattern on the other side of the wall. The foam mediates the impression we make.

And so it is with the communication, which we are able to do through mediums. It may be more direct over time, with development, but the refinement is one of relativity. We must work with the instruments we have, but the message, the essence of what we try to convey, usually succeeds coming through. We stir the stick in the pool and create ripples and you see the ripples. The ripples are an accurate reflection of the consequences of the stick being stirred in the water, but unless you were in the place where the stick was being stirred all you would see on the far side of the lake would be the ripples that it creates and this may be another useful analogy for you.

Hai, again in an effort to make Paul feel secure, gives him an analogy. He tells Eileen:

We give him another analogy of his safety. We place him on the head of an elephant and the elephant treads without fear past the crocodile. If the crocodile should dare to come near it would be unwise.

Note: Paul told Eileen later that he'd been given an image of what Hai described.

Hai continued:

The more you let go, the more you open to spirit influence. This is the essence of all communication. This is the main requirement for communication to take place: to be open, empty; free to allow the influence to express itself. This is no easy task for you, for anybody who wishes to act as a medium for spirit, because you have to put yourself in the background, so to speak, to allow influence to take place.

Can you use every faculty of the medium?

I have to, do I not, to listen to your physical voice and respond to it in a form in which you can clearly hear. We can of course hear what you say in other ways through our spirit faculties, but for the purposes of this communication I use the physical senses.

Can you smell through the medium?

Hai smiles and replies:

I can smell all of you. I can smell through the sense that is Paul's nose, yes.

Can you smell through spirit?

We are aware of the sensations that you experience through smell, but we do not smell in the way that you do.

When you enter Paul, do you enter the whole of his body from head to toe?

No, this is not necessary for communication. But we may vary the degree of occupation if we wish, if it serves a purpose.

Can you gesticulate with your hands?

Yes, we do now sometimes.

*   *   *

On another occasion in the early days of communication Hai had this to say to Eileen:

It's easier, this, when he's totally relaxed. He is not often totally relaxed unfortunately; especially on workdays when it's more difficult. But when he totally relaxes it is much easier for us to communicate and come through. I have more control of his vocal chords at the moment, at this point. This makes communication much easier, and it's more possible to flow without the strain that this sometimes brings. It is momentary. Nevertheless, from quiet moments like this, quiet times in his mind like this, we can build on it and he also can develop a quieter mind in other aspects of his life. It's useful to him not just on these nights, but also when he's at work, using the stillness he needs for this purpose. He is under so much pressure this week that there's not much opportunity to get worked up. So there is some small consolation in this. Not that we would wish him to be under such pressure all the time like this but it has a certain value at times. It makes you focus on what is essential.

*   *   *

One night we just wanted to sit for a short time, because Paul wanted to watch a television programme, Hai commented:

His mind is bothered by the time. You must watch the clock, because of the programme. If you promise to watch the clock his mind will behave itself better.

We'll say fifteen more minutes then.

Very well. We must be careful to arrange things in future to ensure that such things don't disturb his mind. So that if you plan, then his mind can just relax and fall back quietly and at ease and at peace, which enables us to communicate more effectively.

He practises. He is persistent. This is a quality, which is useful to us, this persistence. You attempt much, given the commitments in your lives. There's not as much communication these days as perhaps there was in times gone by because people do not wish, or cannot, or do not see the need or the potential benefit of devoting so much time, effort and energy to communication. But time and effort and energy are what are needed for communication. If it is not put in, there will be no results. But it's difficult for people to commit themselves to this.

Yes, people have such very busy lives now.

They create the business to a certain extent. But conditions do not favour quietness and devotion and dedicated sitting.

Depth and Difficulties of Trance

Our Home Circle members had been discussing how some Healers feel "overlaid" by a spirit person when they give healing. The discussion resulted in Hai being asked the following question.

So, if a taller spirit came to the medium would it be just an expansion of his aura?

This may be so. The sensation of size, whether small or large, may happen with all forms of trance, in all the different conditions of trance, providing the person has some consciousness, of course. However, if they are (smiles) "knocked out," as we seek with Paul, then there is no awareness of size, so the person will not register this.

This "knocking out" then, Hai, is it simply a question of going to a deeper level?

It's a question of taking the person deeper, deeper, so that the mind is no longer conscious of the surroundings or the happenings around it, but can still be used by us to communicate with you.

Do you help with this?

The "knocking out" yes, we help. We do so in the same way in which we've brought about the present condition but we work towards deepening it and removing the obstacle of conscious monitoring which goes on at present.

Each time Paul goes into trance do you help him by degrees to go deeper?

It is not a matter of increment. When he goes "out" it will be a qualitative leap, but the preparation is under way and to that extent all this practice helps.

How will we discern that that has actually happened?

We will tell you when we choose to. You will not notice at first.

I thought there might be a dramatic change?

No, no. I merely mean that the obstacles will have been greatly reduced, as there will not be the conscious monitoring of what we say. His monitoring interferes with what we try to say. It is not a serious impediment but it does restrict what we can achieve. It restricts the detail of what we can give, particularly because the mind, the conscious mind, interferes.

*   *   *

Below is a communication from one of our guest speakers who'd had some difficulty coming through the first time. He explains what it feels like to communicate through a medium in trance.

Are you finding it easier to communicate through Paul now?
Yes I'm finding it easier than it was, yes. But it takes time to find the "right fit."
What does it feel like to communicate through someone like this?
For me it feels frustrating because I can get across so much of myself but not all I would wish to get across. It's filtered, if you like, through the physical body, through the persona of the medium.
Does that mean you can only use certain words because you are using the words in Paul's mind?
I can use his words. I sometimes may slip in one of my own. It's a blend as you have been told before.

*   *   *

Below is an extract of a conversation with WB (spirit scientist.) This took place straight after, Johansen, whose communication is found earlier in this book, had visited us. We'd had more than the usual number of "Guest Speakers" that night and someone commented:

You worked quite hard for us tonight, WB.
Johansen in particular had to work quite hard, as you appreciated, in order to affect the presence.
He didn't have any difficulty once he was through, though.
No, it is precisely that, my dear. It is the early stages of manifesting voice, manifesting personality, which is difficult. Once this is achieved it becomes easier with time and on subsequent occasions. But even so there can be blocks from time to time, as you have noted, because many factors influence and therefore affect our ability to present ourselves in this way. We are dependent upon the feelings of the medium at the time, their health, their disposition of mind at the time and so forth. All these factors have a bearing upon our success.

Chapter 18

Religion, Reality,
the One Mind and Human Life

Hai has been asked many questions about Religion Reality and the One Mind. One night he had the following to say:

The One Mind

Truth is deep, deep without measure, unfathomable. Our minds can never truly embrace it. Our minds can never truly understand because our minds are made for other purposes. They're made for splitting things apart, for naming things, for seeing differences and this is especially true of your minds while you are on the physical plane. But the Reality is one of wholeness; one of unity, one of harmony and it is with the suspension of thought, however brief, that we can really gain an appreciation of this Reality. It is a Reality, which transcends all truths. It transcends all religions because it *is* Reality. It's the Reality, which *is* Truth, which cannot be questioned, which cannot be contradicted. It's like putting your foot into cold water. Your body knows the reality of that. It is beyond question. And this is a poor parallel to give you because your body senses the cold water because of the nature of your body, because you are warmer blooded and what you sense is the contrast of the cold water. So the parallel I give you is poor for this reason. But you take my meaning?

The experience of the One Reality cannot be questioned because it is a concrete experience. It's a concrete reality. Religions are mere ramblings by comparison and I don't say this to disparage religions. But it is one of depth, one of the problems of trying to convey Reality with words. Religions try and succeed to varying degrees to try to portray this Reality. But what they use are words and words are limited, words are restricted. They stand against. They act as labels for things, but they don't stand for the real experience as such. They cannot take the place of the real experience. You talk of the sun and so the sun becomes a word and a useful word at that, because it enables you to talk about the sun. But it cannot enshrine the experience of the sun can it? It merely stands for the sun; and this is the problem that we have with the Truth; the Reality.

This Reality is our Essence. And in essence it is why we show compassion for each other. We share a Common Heart, a Common Mind. It makes no sense to treat each other unfairly, to treat each other without compassion. It is as if we *strike out against ourselves*. We must recognise our Common Heart, our Common Harmony. If there's disharmony instead it's unfortunate, but this disturbance does not reflect Reality. It is rather people disturbing the water, muddying the water, and not seeing the crystal clarity of their Essence, their Common Essence, which they share with each other.

*   *   *

Patience, one of Eileen's healing guides, also had something to say about the One Mind. When answering a question on the subject she told us:

Yes, in the depths in the heart of the flower is a pool of water where the rain has collected and this pool of water contains the mighty ocean and all that is contained therein The Essence of this ocean is Love all-embracing, all-encompassing Love.

Karma and Rebirth

Hai seems most at home when he is answering questions that enable him to provide his answers through philosophy while at the same time teach us to be at one with life. When we start to ask intricate questions and want our answers, "clear cut" Hai often teases us about wanting our "formulae." He loves to give, sometimes quite long, stories, to demonstrate his point.

Can you tell us about very new souls?

New souls are an aspect of the One Mind. No barrier exists between them and the One Mind. You also are part of the One Mind. To talk of new souls is only a matter of convenience, a form of speaking. Because all souls are joined to the One Mind, partake of One Mind, and are aspects of the One Mind.

A new soul, who first comes, if we for the moment accept the idea of new souls, is entering on the road, the journey of discovery. They, at first, are not very aware of their origins and this goes for many of course, even those who are relatively old souls. But life lies in the journey, one of discovery, of rediscovery of your origin, your essence, the One Mind. The One Mind that embraces all is all and shapes all.

There is nothing that you can conceive of that is not part of this Mind, either in life on the earth plane or on the spirit planes: There is nothing that is not contained by this One Mind that does not also partake of its essence. So, these new souls are entering out on a voyage of discovery. They enter on a voyage to rediscover themselves. But, of course, the journey will be long and treacherous, for the road is full of uncertainties, full of experiences, full of discoveries and lost discoveries. But nevertheless, the road goes on and they find themselves slowly but surely and rediscover their spiritual selves, their original essence, their essence in the One Mind.

But, as with anything, in the early stages these souls will be less refined, less mature, while they discover their qualities, their abilities in experiences. They are raw, if you like, in the early stages and it takes time to develop, for them to start to discover themselves and their spiritual heritage.

A member of our circle who was always interested in what Hai had to say on the subjects of Karma and Rebirth had the following questions ready:

Would it be possible for a very old soul to come back to earth into a poor life, poor family, no education or very little education, and if it is possible, what will happen to that soul when they arrive in the spirit land if their education has been limited and their whole life limited? Will it restrict them from moving on faster than they might do otherwise?

It depends upon the development at the time when you enter the physical plane. You know that you've all had many lives before.

Therefore, the stage of development when you achieve the earth plane again may vary and therefore you advance through your experience. But when you return to the spirit plane you are the sum of your experience, your development.

Would that be apparent to the person immediately on returning to spirit?

No, but in the fullness of time when the seed ripens.

So, for someone who has had a poor life and limited education, will it take them longer to move on in the spirit world and to be aware of their full development?

Not when they return to the spirit world.

Is it possible for a new soul to come to earth and be born into a loving family and have a nice life?

Yes. What does the first experience matter? In the fullness of time all experiences are possible.

Would a new soul be likely to make the best use of an experience like that?

Would a new soul be in the best position to make the best use of a poor life, a harsh life, any more so than an easy life? So what does it matter? A life is a life and we must make of it what we can.

So, anyone, in any kind of a life on earth, could be a young or old soul?

The experiences are varied and each experience may suit the needs of the soul for this rebirth. There are so many permutations, but each permutation allows a close fit for what is needed by the soul.

Is this why some of the books report that some people who go over to spirit may feel unimportant and believe they've done very little with their life, but nevertheless, have beautiful colourful auras? Does this indicate that they are old evolved souls?

Yes, just so.

I know we can't have hard and fast answers, Hai and it's all very complicated.

It is simple. It is simple. Your minds make it complicated. Your minds make complications where none exist.

I suppose that's partly due to things being passed on down through the ages and beliefs in society and people talking about there being no justice in the world.

This was just the question Hai was searching for as it gave him the opportunity to tell us one of his "stories."

Hai's Story

You want to explore the swamp? Well, you go into this swamp and you see this beautiful flower. This beautiful flower has four delicate white petals and as you look at its centre you see it has a purple ring at the centre where the petals join the stem. As you look at the centre, the heart of the plant, you see the beautiful gold centre. Is this not a beautiful flower, a beautiful flower, yes? So you decide that you will have a close look at this flower. You decide that you will dissect it to more fully appreciate it. So you get your little penknife out and you carefully, because you do not want to hurt this flower, carefully take off its petals, one by one, and you look at them and you decide: "Ah! I had better measure how much white there is and how much purple there is. This must be *very important, very important*." So this is what we do. And we notice the curve of the petals and think: "Ah! This must be significant. Yes, this must be *very important*." So we carefully measure the curve of the petals. Then we look at the centre, the centre of the flower and we see all these stamens and we say: "Ah! It must be *very important, very important*, to know how many there are." So we set to with our penknife and we cut them out one by one. But these stamens are so small, so delicate. It's very difficult to separate them, very difficult to set them apart. We carry on, and before we know where we are, we have a whole load of them and we start to think: "Ah! We must count them. This must be *very important* to know how many there are." And so we set them out in a row and we count them. But we get halfway through counting them and we lose count and so we get frustrated. We start to worry: "Oh! I must start again. This must be important to know." So we start again, but again we lose count. We become frustrated with this and then somebody passes us by and says; "What are you doing?" We explain. "Ah!" he says, "Well you count the stamens, but you have not done anything with the stem yet, so what are you going to do with the stem?"

"Ah!" we say, "well, right, we had better examine that as well." So we pull the stem out of the ground and we cut it down the middle and we look at it very carefully, very carefully, and we notice that it's made up of different compartments. So we think: "Ah! This must be important." So we document these compartments. Yes? And we remember: "Ah! We have not counted these stamens yet!" So we go back to count these stamens. Eventually we get the right number and this man comes back again and says: "Where are you up to?" And we say to him: "Now, we have counted all the stamens, we have documented all the petals, all the features of the petals. We've documented the compartments of the stem." And he says to you: "Well, you have missed out one of the most important parts; what of the root?"

"Ah! We forgot this," we say. So we take our trowel and we dig deep down in the soil to pull out the roots. We separate all these roots from the soil and we count the branches of the roots. We measure them and we measure the important bigger ones and the little ones. Yes? And then this man comes back and he says: "Ah! You have finished then, have you?" "Yes," we say, proud of ourselves, "we have finished. We have filled all this paper. We have all these measurements. We have now got the *essence* of this flower." And he says: "Have you indeed? Where is this flower you first saw now? What have you done to it with your mind?"

You understand this story? Not only has the *essence* of the flower been lost, *its heart has been pulled asunder*. The **truth** is known through here (pressing to his heart). *If we seek it with our minds we lose it*. Our minds are tools. We must be careful with our tools, because our tools can do damage as well as good. The truth is an insight, not gained by splitting hairs.

*　　　　　*　　　　　*

When we'd taken a few minutes to absorb Hai's story, someone commented:

We were given minds though, Hai.

Just so and so they are our tools. We must ensure that they serve us and do not hinder us. There is a time for analysis, for splitting things up. But when it comes to the Divine Truth, **this is not the way.** When it comes to the experience of life, and in the joy of the Now, joy of the moment, **this is not the way.**

I try to just accept things, but unfortunately, sometimes my mind gets working.

The Phoenix, when it arose from the ashes, flew to the heights of the sky, the beautiful firmament. Then, all of a sudden, it started to think: "Wait a minute! I died! I was ash! How can I be flying in the firmament in this way?" And, it started to think so much about this problem, that without realising it, it stopped flying and fell onto the earth and died. Our minds can strangle us, can strangle the joy of life, if we allow them. Therefore, we must bring them to our service and not allow them to be our master.

So should we just accept things as they are then; life as it is?

It depends what you wish. It depends what you seek. If you seek the Ultimate you will not find it in your concepts and words. If you seek peace you will not find it in your concepts and words. If you wish to build a bridge in your physical plane then you will need to use your mind and your mathematics and your other concepts to build that bridge. But that is for a bridge not for the joy of life, the essence of life.

Is it easier to think in the way you've just described when you go the spirit world, or is it more difficult if you have not come to terms with it here first?

You should seek this way of thinking here and not think about whether it is easier or more difficult in the spirit land. You are here. You are living here in the Now so you must live in the Now, this moment, with a peaceful mind.

*   *   *

Development in the Spirit World and the Reason for Coming to Earth

The night began with a simple question about Shakespeare:

Hai, do people like Shakespeare continue with their writing in spirit, or do they do other things?

They may do other things, they may also continue to persevere with their writing or other artistic ability, which they have had on the earth plane. We are not limited in this and therefore, it is up to them what they choose to do, whether they wish to continue to refine their art or whether they wish to develop in other ways to broaden their abilities and their horizons.

If you do continue with the same thing as you did on the earth plane, would that stop you from improving yourself?

Yes it could because you become too narrow, too focused, which is what you imply, Tom. You are correct. It is sometimes more important, at the opportune moment, to broaden out other skills and abilities in order to become a more "rounded" person. Therefore, all these things have their place and their time but it may be more important to move on, as you suggest and develop other abilities.

Someone else asked:
How does this transition, this moving on thing work?
This moving on thing; what do you mean Andy?
Well, do you have to sit an exam?
No there is no exam to be sat. There is a *knowing* when the time has come. There is a *knowing* that you are ready to move through, to progress, to the next realm. It is more gradual than when you are catapulted into the spirit land once more (at death) from your physical body. There is opportunity, to visit you might say, the other realms when you are in the spirit realms, to sense and test them out, to acclimatise yourself to them. Therefore, the transition may be more gradual, more gentle.
If we can evolve in spirit why do we bother coming down here into the physical?

This amused Hai and he replied:

For the bother of it (laughs.) Yes there are things that you experience in this realm (earth) that you cannot experience in other realms. It is what you would call in your language, the "school of hard knocks," (laughs again) yes, the "school of hard knocks." But this is a good school for learning things. "Hard Knock School," is good for knocking us into shape. It is not so easy to learn some of these things in the spirit lands, quicker learning in school of hard knocks.

You can't experience pain in the same way, in the same sense within the spirit lands, and you do not experience separation in the same way. You do not have to be subjected to the ageing of a physical body in the same way. You do not have to be subjected to change in the physical world that you experience, in the same way. All these things are useful tools, useful experiences for learning. So you are subjected to physical change both in your physical body and in your environment. You learn that your environment and your physical body, what you hold most dear to yourself, is not fixed, is not changeless. Therefore, this makes you go in search to seek the Changeless within the changing world;

Changeless within your own changing physical body and this sets you on the spiritual quest.

Those who seek to preserve their body as if, (smiling) they would pickle it while still living, are unfortunately on a misguided path, for they hang on to the externals whereas the externals are forever changing. It is like grasping sand in the desert; as fast as you grasp it, the tighter you hold it; the more it slips through your fingers. This is true is it not? So if you try and preserve your youth and beauty it is a forlorn task for it still sifts through your fingers. And even if you manage to preserve the outer skin, the outer shell, you will continue to age with your experience *within* yourself, which gives the lie to your physical smooth skin (smiles.) But more importantly, this fact of the ageing experience fosters the spiritual quest, fosters the seeking, the realisation of the eternal within you. In spite of all the change there is an eternal core, the changelessness of youth and beauty. But if your eyes are fixed to the mirror and the image of the reflection of your skin, this is a distraction and you will be distracted from your spiritual quest and what is truly important in life.

Can you experience fear and anxiety in the spirit world?

No not in the way that you experience it. You can experience emotion in the spiritual lands, the experience, the pain of emotion, loss, anguish, and grief. It is not emotionless and in fact it is more of a problem to contain and manage your emotions, but there is not the same difficulty regarding fear and anxiety though there can be some regret.

Is not one experience on the earth sufficient for us to learn about pain?

Well, we are not quick learners; we are slow learners often. Like a child in the classroom who feels; "I do not want to be in this classroom I want to go home," (laughs) so we think sometimes; "I don't want to be here, I don't want to learn these lessons, I want to go home." So we go home and the wise man at the gate says; "Ok so you are home and you can stay home for a bit but because you did not learn your lessons you are going to have to go back again to the school."

How many times do we have to come to the earth?

There is no fixed multiplication.

Is there an average time then before we are allowed to stay?

It is not a case of allowing, Tom. It is a case of whether you think you have finished your schooling.

Eileen commented:

I personally think there is no end to all this and unless we achieve enlightenment we will never stop coming back. Is this true, Hai?

I suggest you develop *tranquil spirit* (the name of our home.)

Hai laughs and continues:

You can stop coming back when the time is come. When the time is right you stop coming back, yes.

It was obvious Hai was listening to Davia in the background. He continued to laugh and added:

He says, (referring to Davia) you never truly avoid coming back, even when you do not need to come back, because they subject you to coming back on a Friday night to listen to people singing in the dark. *
(Laughs again heartily)

*Note: This was a joke in reference to our singing when we sit in the dark, singing in an attempt to raise energies, ever hopeful for some physical phenomena to occur.

Human Life

Hai had the following to say on the "Human Ego"

We assume or take upon ourselves the burden of responsibility for other people, of certain conditions around us. This can be a sort of arrogance, because we inflate ourselves. It's a problem, which many people have because their egos are strong and because their egos are strong, sometimes, they can attribute more to themselves than is necessary or desirable. There are many forms of arrogance so it may be that people experience or suffer from some forms of arrogance and not others. One form of arrogance is to assume that we are always right. That our opinions are always right, and correct or our opinions are better than those of others. This is one form of arrogance.

But another form of arrogance, in a sense, is to focus too much on ourselves, on our responsibility, or sense of responsibility, our role, our purpose, our individuality, our being. We can overdo such things. We all of course, need a sense of responsibility. That is right and correct.

Without it, that would be a great error. But, we can exaggerate our view of ourselves, our view of our degree of responsibility, our view of our duty.

These can all be exaggerated to our detriment and the detriment of others. So, they speak of duty, for instance. Duty is an honourable virtue. But if the ego becomes too involved with this duty, this honourable virtue becomes oppressive, becomes a problem to us. And in fact it cuts us off from our spiritual heritage, rather than being an aid to link to it.

This ego thing is not a simple matter, as you see. The ego is subtle, it is tacky, it is slippery, and we must be wary of it: Openness, directness, compassion, patience, and endurance. These are all worthwhile virtues, which should be practiced, not as virtues, but, because we have learnt to see the person before us and these virtues are naturally evoked in us because we see the person, we see their essence, their soul, their worth. And it is therefore, then, that these virtues naturally are called forth in us not because we practiced these virtues like some skills, which we've learnt. I do not say any of this is easy. But this is the way forward.

Parents and Children

One visitor to our circle asked Hai's advice on a matter regarding her child whom she was concerned about. She commented:

Society places most of our children's problems on parents.

And parents must accept some responsibility. It is true. But that is not the whole story, is it? Your children are born from your genes, but they are not carbon copies of you. They are shaped and moulded to their own individuality. They must work with their bodies, their physical selves. Their experience is unique. Their experience is different to yours. We must be careful of imposing our frameworks upon them. They must grow and learn from their own experience, as difficult as that is for us as parents, watching from the outside, so to speak. We have our part to play but we must not overdo it. We must give them freedom and space for growth.

But sometimes when they make mistakes it often affects the parents.

We all make mistakes. We have to make mistakes, to grow, to learn. If nobody made any mistakes nobody would learn anything worthwhile. We can guide, we can advise, but people have to live their own lives and make their own mistakes. We cannot live their lives for them, nor would we want to, nor should it be so. We must live our lives and they theirs, though we share a Common Heart, a Common Meaning, a Common Purpose, a Common Mind even.

Efficiency

The following conversation took place after a visitor asked Hai's advice on a work issue. She commented:

Employers usually want things done in a certain way in the name of efficiency.

Efficiency. I tell you, if the prime directive of the One Mind was efficiency, it would long ago have achieved its final ends. Life is not about efficiency. We find ways to do things, which are helpful, supportive, which do not waste our resources. But there are bigger goals, greater goals, more important goals than efficiency. Perhaps your time has lost this point. Perhaps your time focuses too much on efficiency. Where is the human heart in this process of efficiency? This is the question. If the efficiency serves the human heart, all well and good, if it does not, efficiency is non-efficiency.

But we are put on the earth. We have to feed and clothe ourselves so people have to find work, to do that we have to show that we are efficient. That's our reality, Hai, of the way it is, to survive.

Yes, but who creates the ground rules to this efficiency? Who creates the boundaries? Do they have a human interest at heart? And so, if the people who create efficiency systems do not have the human heart at the essence, at the heart of their own thoughts, it will go wrong. It will go wrong and you must guard against being caught up in the flow.

I know what you are saying, Hai, but for ordinary people, who can't get a job easily, they can't help but become caught up in efficiency.

There must be compromises, we know. We must make compromises. But what I say to you is that we must not make a god out of efficiency. The Romans made a god out of efficiency to an extent. They made a god out of power and we can see where that led.

This time Eileen laughed. She responded:
Paul (the medium) has a high regard for the Romans, Hai.
Hai smiled:

He is being educated. Your human societies should evolve; yet there are dangers. Because if you do not constantly face forward and walk forward, you may slip back. Your politicians think too much of ideas. Ideas are necessary, but you must be careful that they do not turn into shackles. And they should ask themselves: "If we put this idea into action what are the consequences? Where will it lead? Will it produce a greater good at the end of the day rather than doing nothing? Is the good, which it will produce, justified by the harm it might also produce?" These are the questions of a wise sage, of a wise ruler.

Hunting

One night there was some discussion about the Bill to stop hunting and that it didn't appear to be getting enough government support. Some people thought that this might be due to a fear of losing votes. Expecting Hai to condemn hunting without reservation; some of the group were somewhat surprised by his answer:

As ever it was, as ever it was. The rulers take account of the different pressures, which they are under, of the different needs of the different groups in society. This is inevitable, but they should plough slowly on, firmly on along the course, which they know is right. It is better to win people's minds and hearts though, than to impose things on them. This is not efficient of course, but it's a better way, a more lasting way. If people seek to impose their will on others, even though their cause is just, they become contaminated, because a just cause for them becomes an egotistical cause. They do violence to it.

Birds, Zoo's and Dolphins

One night one of our group members commented that he had stopped keeping birds because he was concerned that to keep them in captivity was unkind. The questions continued and expanded to other animals. Hai's response to these questions may surprise you. He began by replying to the first comment about birds. He told us:

Birds are meant to fly, yes, so this is how it should be.

Another member commented:

You can keep birds in an aviary so that they can fly but they cannot fly far.

It is about the quality of life, which they may experience. Even though they cannot fly, perhaps as much as in the wild, the bond grows and develops between them and the humans who look after them. This bond of love provides a quality that they cannot have in the wild state generally. So this is not so simple. But birds should be able to fly; they were born to fly.

In the spirit lands there are not these dilemmas because all have their safety, all can have their liberty. There is not the fear between animals and the spirit people. So bonds may form. Bonds based upon previous relationships or based upon new relationships. Animals have their liberty but they may form bonds with people and this is as it should be because we are all of the spirit, all of the One Mind. All animals also are within the love of the One Mind so it is right that there should be comradeship among us. It is possible to make a big thing of animals being free in their wild state yet not recognise the emotional bond between they and us.

What are your views on keeping animals in zoos?

This depends upon the animal; its natural state and to what extent that state can be recreated within such an environment. The manner of obtaining the animal also has some bearing on this. Some animals are manifestly not suited to being contained in such an environment. There is neither the space nor the natural conditions of their life to provide them with so they would best not be kept in such a state; but providing it is an environment that approaches their natural condition, others may be happy living in a zoo. Nevertheless, the dignity of the animals should be, above all else, maintained. They are our brothers and should be viewed as such. Reach out with your love to the animals. Reach out.

A member of the group commented on the beauty of dolphins. Hai responded:

Yes, they are lovely creatures dolphins, beautiful creatures, and intelligent spiritual beings.
They always seem happy. Are they more evolved than other animals?
They are very evolved, more evolved than most animals.
Are they more evolved than humans?
No not more than humans, but not far away from humans in many ways.
What other animals would you say are evolved?
Well, you know these I'm sure, but there are the pandas the gorillas, chimpanzees, or orang-utan. Bears also very evolved.

There was some discussion about the various skills of animals and one member commented:
I think every animal has its own skill, Hai.
Yes it is true. We should respect the skills of these different animals; we should respect their abilities for we would all be found wanting, in certain situations, whereas these animals would survive.

Multiple Marriages:
Hai's Joke

A circle member referred to someone he knew who'd had a good many husbands in this life. He asked:
Who will she be with when she passes over? She's had about nine husbands.

Hai's answer was quick and to the point:
Number 10. For if she has gone through so many husbands in this lifetime, then she's unsettled and is still looking for her ideal husband, ideal relationship; therefore, number 10. But you know she may renew relationships when she is on our side. She may have more appreciation for relationships. But a person with so many relationships may have much to learn about relationships perhaps. But sometimes because of the nature of life and the nature of way of living this sometimes makes relationships difficult; circumstances of relationships make it difficult.

But, who knows? She will have a lot to reflect upon. She will have a lot to tell others and reflect upon as she walks the planes in the spirit lands. She could find herself employed by Henry* as an aid to share remembrances and experiences with those others who would wish to hear.

* Henry is a spirit counsellor. His communication can be found in Part two.

Is it true though, Hai, that if someone loved two people on the earth plane it is possible for them all to be together in the spirit land?
There is no reason why this should not be case, no reason at all. But you know things move on, things change. Sometimes people may stay together. Truly,—love souls you might say. Other times they might say; well we love each other, we have enjoyed each other greatly but we must move on, we must change in some way to enable both of us to continue to grow; such souls may part in perfect bliss of love and may indeed join together later in time. So you should not look at things too rigidly for we are all embraced by the One Heart, within the One Heart. Nothing is separate, nothing is cast aside, all is embraced, all are embraced; none are outside the Love, the One Heart.

*   *   *

Laughter

One night Hai was asked:
What importance has laughter in life?
It is important to life. It is important to find joy in life. I know it is not easy but it is important to hang on to joy. It is good to be joyful despite the pressures in life. Seriousness has its place also; our lives must be balanced.

Chapter 19

Conversations with the Phoenix group

Communication, as we have demonstrated, has not always been serious philosophy; even Hai has many humorous moments and regularly shows his human side. The following took place during the very early days of communication when Eileen and I would sit alone. She would chat and joke with Hai just as though they were old friends. Here is a small snippet of their conversations:

Friends talking:

One night Hai told Eileen:

It is funny sitting here sensing familiar sensations from the past, when I was in my body. It is a strange sensation, a heavy sensation, but not unpleasant to feel the old familiar sensations. Not that I would want to return permanently of course. No, a little experience is enough, for now, from where I am. I prefer my present conditions to a return to earth.

And on another he commented:

He's cheeky. (Referring to Paul the medium) He asks me what I'm doing, just sitting here quietly while not speaking. I will speak when I am ready. If he was a bit quieter I could speak more readily, but his mind still chatters from time to time.

Eileen decided to ask Hai some grandfatherly advice:

They've asked me to operate the organ in church, Hai, but I'm afraid of pressing the wrong buttons.

Better that than to sing in the choir. You must not think me too unkind.

Oh, I know I can't sing.

I joke with you. I also could not sing, as you have witnessed tonight. A hum was my best effort.

Well I plan, when I go to the spirit world, to take singing lessons.

Yes, this will be possible. You will do so if you wish. We are able to do many things that we could not do while on the earth. We can develop skills that we would have liked to develop, which we had no opportunity to develop. So if you wish to sing you shall sing. You can be assured of that.

I'd like to be able to play the piano as well as Liberace.

Well, you could practise on this organ, couldn't you?

On another occasion Eileen commented:

You were singing another song just before, Hai.

No. It was not a song. It was reminiscent of my language—well, in my earthly lifetime. It was not a song this time.

Last time you said that coming back here had reminded you of that song. Can't you sing the same kind of songs in the spirit world as you did when on the earth plane?

We do indeed. I was merely using a phrase, a turn of phrase. Being back in the body reminded me again of times on earth. Reminded me of the circumstances that I've been in. Reminded me of the things I used to do. So singing was one of them. Not a profession, you understand!

A bit like me?

Yes. We would not know who was the most in need of training.

You or me?

Training in fact is optimistic, is it not? You do not have the quality of voice. But, as I have said, these restrictions, these limitations, are removed once in the spirit. If you wish to sing, you shall and there will be training for you if you require it—if you want it. You will have the equipment, which is necessary. On earth we don't all have the equipment to sing melodiously.

*   *   *

Members of our Home Circle also enjoy the same comfortable familiarity with our spirit group. One night someone asked Hai:

I've been reading a book, Hai, and I am curious to know how you would respond. If someone said ninety-nine guides out of one hundred talked a load of rubbish, how would you respond to them?

Hai was amused and replied:
> It is fortunate I am one of out of a hundred. (Laughter)
> *That was a short answer.*
> But swift answer, best answer.

And our guest speakers have not been without their humour. One spirit visitor was asked:

Have you visited us before at these meetings?
> I've been on the sidelines, but this is the first time I've managed to talk to you. It's a good show. Free, as well! You are most generous not wanting payment.

Even Isleen, who is probably one of the more serious members of our spirit group, often displays her less serious side. One night just prior to starting our meditation she explained to a new visitor:

> I am the lady of the group, though I must not claim sole title for there are others also in our group, you understand. But I tend to be the one to come forward to represent them. I have been spoken of as being softly spoken—you understand, my new friends—yes, to the point that Davia mocks me and says I will send people to sleep one day—but you must put up with me, yes.
> *You are using the energy well.*
> Thank you, my friend; flattery will get you everywhere.

*　　　　　*　　　　　*

The members of our spirit group have always been reluctant to talk about themselves and their last incarnation on earth unless they've felt that by disclosing parts of their lives there have been lessons for us all to learn. This has been especially so with Hai who has only given us short snippets of his life, either when he's been asked a direct question, or if it related to something he wished to talk about. He has often told us that we must only judge him by his message and not who he was on earth.

We have already given you extracts from conversations with WB, our spirit scientist, Carol and Lopaz. Here are a few short extracts from conversations with Hai and the other members of the group:

Conversation with Hai

Was it a very serious life as a Buddhist monk?
You would think so and it was serious much of the time, in a sense. But our quest was serious. People generally did not come into the monastery lightly. Though, for some, they were pushed in perhaps. It was an austere life but we had some sense of fun also. Yet, for all the difference both in the manner of life and in the difference in time in which we have lived on this earth, there is a commonality in the existence that we have experienced. For all the change and differences the human experience remains the same as such.

Life, life's routine—a daily pattern. We had farming to do. We had work to do about the monastery, as well as the business of "sitting" which was our central purpose. Enlightenment was our central aim, but we had a routine of daily life nevertheless. The routine itself was seen as a way to achieve enlightenment. There was no serious distinction, between sitting in the meditation hall and working in the field or about the chores, which we engaged in around the monastery, because the essence of life is everywhere. The essence of life is "at one" whatever activity we are engaged in. It is there—we are in it. We share a common core.

On another occasion Hai was asked:

Did you live a harmonious life?
Harmony?—In the "back-biting," yes. Monks are human beings like all human beings, they have their strengths; they have their failings. There was a harmony—an overall harmony, but there was competition also. We had differences of opinion, there was conflict, but

in spite of this there was indeed harmony. There was a structure to our daily life, a simplicity, which encouraged, facilitated this harmony, this stillness of mind but not all achieved this stillness—not all. Some came to the monastery for different reasons, for pragmatic reasons sometimes. So we had a variety of people in the monastery and where you get a variety of people, you get the full range of the human condition.

On one occasion Hai volunteered:

    We did much work with the plants in my monastery.

    Did you grow your own vegetables?

    Yes our own vegetables and we grew plants, which we simply enjoyed also.

One evening Eileen was interested to know:

    Did they have women in your dynasty?

    There were nuns, Buddhist nuns.

    Were they high up in the hierarchy?

    I would not say so because it was to do with the times the culture of the times. They had high respect—those who became wise—those who became enlightened.

Another female member of the group made a joke about women's superiority and Hai gave this interesting reply:

    To the extent that you make a thing of your superiority, you undermine your superiority.

The questions continued:

    Is your home in the spirit world, compact?

    It is compact. It's not a rambling house; it is rather a small retreat.

    Are you happy there?

    Yes, it suits my needs. I have simple needs. I merely need somewhere that has quiet, to which I can retreat periodically, to collect my thoughts, to meditate upon the reality, upon the spirit world, upon the work we do across the worlds—I mean the planes. Planes, worlds, call them what you will, they are only terms, only words to signify a reality—a reality which words ultimately cannot encompass nor describe in adequate terms.

*   *   *

One night Hai started the meeting with the following words:

I wish I could share with you the joy, the experience on a regular basis, living as I do in the land of spirit, a great joy of heart, which is not always present in the physical condition.

What have you been doing since we last spoke?

I am often in my dwelling and I contemplate the spirit world. I contemplate our tasks, our venture with you. I contemplate much.

Are there issues in the spirit world as there are on earth?

There are not the same issues in the sense in which you have issues. I was rather referring to the essence, the life within the spirit world, the loving vibrations, the harmonious vibrations, the expression of the spiritual within the forms of the spirit world.

*   *   *

When our dog started barking and Eileen had to go to him, Hai had the following to say on her return:

Well, little dogs are easily disturbed. We had animals in the monastery; we have little dogs in the monastery. We have cats in the monastery also. Dogs chase cats, yes.

Did they breed all over the place?

Well we had a few.

Were they tame?

Oh yes. We looked after them. Yes.

Hai then referred to our recent Christmas celebrations and commented:

Your Christmas celebrations are hard work. We found festivals in the monastery in China hard work for we had to prepare for festivities, it was expected by people; but good fun also.

Did you get involved in preparing for these festivities, Hai?

Oh yes, oh yes. We were centre stage.
Were they religious festivals you refer to?
Yes and festivals of the countryside—folklore festivals.
Was it this time of year?
Well we have festivity at all times of year but also around this time
of year like you.

*   *   *

On another occasion Hai was asked:

Do you think you will come back again?
No, I do not think so but we must never say, never, for we do not
know. It may be that I might be required to come back, to move back
into your world and I would do so willingly if that were the case.

How do you present yourself now to the rest of the spirit group, Hai?

There was a silence. Eileen asked if the silence was meant to be telling
us something. Hai answered:

Well, it tells you that we do not need to have this clear form; we do
not need to have this signature for we have another signature, a
spiritual signature that reflects our essence.
Do you just appear as a light then?
Yes, we could just appear as light, with its own signature, yes.
And do the spirit group still know it's you?
Yes.

Conversation with Isleen:

When Isleen was asked about her life, she replied:

We were born into an Irish family as you know and we worked the
land. There were a lot of us, a big family. I was viewed as a bit odd
because I had these fancies of connecting with spirit, so this did not go
down very well all the time. But we must do our own thing, mustn't
we. We must find our own expression and not worry about thoughts
of others about it, yes. And so, we lived a peaceful life, happy life

overall. It was hard at times but we did well, we survived, we thrived, we were happy in the countryside. I married and had children, lived also on a farm while I was married.

We lived in the 1800s. I had a nun who was a friend of mine who wore one of those big hats.

Are you still a medium in the spirit realm, Isleen?

I still act as a medium in the spirit realm for those who wish to make contact with those from other realms, though the barriers between our realms are not as solid, as fixed as perhaps they are for you in relative terms.

Conversation with Davia

Eileen had previously asked Hai if Davia's name was correct because names ending in A are usually female. Hai indicated that the name was not important. He explained that the name, Davia, was not an exact replica of the one he'd had on the earth plane but was a name Davia had become attached to. Apparently he likes to make much of the *"ia"* sound at the end of the name. Something he puts to great effect when communicating with us.

The following communication starts on a quiet note and Davia explains how he was drawn to the spirit group. He then changes his style and offers us a taste of his humour, which is in "top form." Unfortunately though, words can only provide a flavour of his humour; Davia must be heard,—to be fully appreciated. He told us:

I was born on your earth plane in Papua New Guinea Sometime ago now. I lived a simple life but a happy life.

How did you come to join this group?

We are drawn to each other; we have an affinity. We learn also that there is an enterprise to be undertaken. We can "apply" if you like. We join with spirits of similar mind who wish to engage in the enterprise. We are of like mind.

Would you like to share some spirit philosophy with us?

Be calm in your approach to life. Be tranquil in your approach to life. Don't get ruffled. (Smiles) Let the others get ruffled if they really want to.

The questions continued and Davia's more humorous side began to show.

Davia, in your country, did you have a religion?
Oh yes we had much religion, we had lots of religion, we had religion coming out of the ears.
Did your religion allow more than one wife?
What good is a religion that didn't allow it?
I thought your race might have been short of men?
No.
Did you live off the fruit or did you grow things?
Well we did some collecting of food in the forests and jungle. We also grew a little and we hunted as well—the animals.
Did you ever get honey?
Yes, you could get honey from them mean bees but you got to be careful, you could "smoke" them and they go dopey—then you can get the honey. *

Note: Davia had explained on a previous occasion that he would put something in the hives to cause smoke and dope the bees.

And on another occasion Davia was asked:

Would all the people in your tribe have been laid-back like you, Davia?

This gave Davia the opportunity he was looking for to begin his repartee:

Well, the place helped you know, Eileen, the place helped you to feel laid-back but, as with all peoples, there is much variation. Much variation in the ability for *relaxation*, you understand, because some people's characters are not predisposed to being laid-back, to *relaxing*. It depends upon character also but it is a fact that if you create the right circumstances on the earth plane you will find that there are more people laying back and falling over than would be the case otherwise. So if you create right conditions, you create the possibility of more people being laid-back. If you create wrong conditions fewer people are laid-back. Yes, instead you get lots of people rushing forward all the time, tripping over their feet.

So have you been really tested out on earth, Davia, in a situation where you might get more stressed-up?

(Laughing) I know were you are coming from, Eileen. You're trying to get me to volunteer to come back here because I have not had the *full* experience of the earth plane and you want me to put myself under stressful conditions to see if I can be laid-back or not.

Yes that's what I mean.

Well I am not taking that bait. (laughter) I've been there, I've done it, I've got your tee-shirt as you say because I'm laid-back, because I've been through all this. I've seen it; I've done it all. I know it all and therefore I am *here*, I'm not *there*. Nor do I want to come back *there* because in spite of your reluctance to come up *here*, I can assure you it is a lot better than down *there*. Yeah.

When everyone, including Davia, had finished laughing, Eileen answered:

Well you made a lot out of that one didn't you, Davia?
Well that's my skill I think you have recognised.
It is and I have. (Much more laughter)

Chapter 20

Hui Hai the Buddhist Abbot

As time went on, we became aware that Hai's first name was Hui and that he'd eventually become the Abbot in the monastery where he lived. We were also aware that during his time on earth many of his teachings had been recorded, some of which were later translated into the English language.

One member of our circle had attempted to read one of these books; however, as it was full of Buddhist terminology he'd found the book difficult to understand. One night Eileen commented on this to Hai. He replied:

Yes, but you must remember that whatever you read in that book is only another way of me saying what I say to you here. Nothing in that book is different from what I say to you here but it is expressed in a different form and therefore may give you another insight into things, from a different angle, if you like. But when you read it, if you think of what you have heard here when we've discussed these things, what you read should become clearer.

Eileen asked whether Hai was aware of the content of the book we were currently writing, on his behalf. He answered:

Yes, we know what you are writing.
Do you have any recommendations or comments, Hai?
We would think emphasis, overall theme, yes, running through the book, running through all what you write in the book should be about helping to see how the person may develop spiritually and how they may develop in their spiritual connections with the spiritual world. We

do not say so much what you call psychic development but this may be "off spin," but what we say is we would like people to know, to experience, lasting deeper spiritual awareness: awareness of a spiritual world, spiritual backdrop, aspect to life within their own daily life. So we would like to think that we could help them appreciate this, to develop an awareness of this: To develop an awareness that there is more to life than the physical forms that they see and to develop an appreciation of the spiritual reality, the spiritual essence behind and within these forms. Yes.

Do we need to include anything extra?

Well, it is more to do with "spin" you put on the book, yes. The material you have is fine, but if you keep in mind this theme as you write, as you revise your writings, this may help you. But truly we wish to feel, to be experienced as us *speaking from our hearts,* to reflect our love: To reflect the love we give out that we wish to share with you all: To experience a mutual love, a mutual sharing, a togetherness, a oneness within the words of this book, yes.

It's difficult picking out the most appropriate "Guest Speaker" out of so many.

Ah, you should not over-worry too much because if you take out one bit that might be the bit that some individual over on the far side of earth would be inspired by, yes. Someone else might not like it too much but someone might be helped by it. So you cannot please everyone at the same time, like you say. But also it is that *one* word, *one* sentence, *one* story will inspire someone where it does not inspire others, but if it inspires one it has done its work.

*   *   *

If you read Paul's introduction at the beginning of this book you will know that for many years both Paul and Eileen were very much involved with their local Spiritualist church. However, Paul, if asked, would usually describe himself as Buddhist, and Eileen would say she did not belong to any religion. Nevertheless, it is natural that we will draw people to us who have an interest in communication with the spirit world and so have also belonged to, or at least visited a Spiritualist church. When several people who call themselves Spiritualists meet in this way it can occasionally give the group a "feel" almost, that a meeting of Spiritualists is taking place. One night, when this was particularly apparent Hai told us:

You should not label us, these activities, as to do with Spiritualism, or anything else for that matter, for they are simply communications between dear friends, some in spirit, some on the earth plane.

Eileen responded:
We don't do that, Hai.
We know this but we reinforce it, emphasise it and agree with you, for if this happens it then becomes yet another "ism." And when we talk of Spiritualism we talk simply of communication between those in spirit and those on the earth plane. If you look at the philosophies and teaching of what you call Spiritualism, you will find variation. You cannot fix what we do here in a mould. And what we urge upon you, as we have always urged upon you, is to use your own judgment in listening to these communications. To take what is true and good in your own discernment and hold to it as you would hold to any truth, which you take upon yourself. But if anything should seem out of kilter, unwise, unsure in your discernment, then you should put it to one side for we are not offended. It is your divine right to use your free will wisely.

We draw upon the religions of all faiths, of all cultures and we have brought many people to you from diverse cultures and faiths and we do this deliberately. You may find a current, a core, an essence of truth running through but they will express these truths, this essence, in their own way and so some refer to the Godhead or God, some will refer to Allah: I refer to the One Mind—Suchness, but we all speak of the Divine Essence, the Spiritual Essence.

Why Hai Communicates Now

One member, referring to the earlier discussion about Hai's writings when on the earth plane, asked:

Is that one of the reasons why you want to write another book now?

Yes we wish to make the teaching accessible to others, many others. We wish to make it accessible to people of all religion and none. We would like to make it accessible in words of your time, in manner, in mode of your time, yes. We wish to reach out with loving heart to people of your day, your time. In reaching out to people of your day, your time with loving heart our hearts connect in the beauty of mutual love.

There was a pause; Hai continued:

Why cannot people reach out? Why cannot people reach out with hearts of mutual love, my friends? Why can they not look each other in the eye and find love in their hearts for the other person? Why is this not so, my friends?

So much beauty staring at you with eyes, yet there are many who cannot do this, who do not do this, who will not do this. For they often have preconceptions about others. They often have opinions about other genders, yes, but if they could only be open, if they could only be free of prejudices, of opinions, of distortions. If they could see people for whom they are. If we offer a person, another person, something positive, a sign, a symbol of our own good faith, of our own love for them, of our own wish to work with them in brotherhood: This undermines the seeds of evil: This undermines the seeds of hatred and revulsion and will bring about a revolution, a transmutation of hatred into love.

Chapter 21

A Selection of Blessings

Monsignor Robert Hugh Benson

(Spirit communicator in the book "Life in the Spirit World" Anthony Borgia)

So it remains for me to finish for the night and resume my former occupation. So I give you my blessing. I will give you the blessing of all of us from the spirit lands who are gathered here tonight and the blessing of the Great Spirit, the One Mind, which is behind all and sustains all. We wish you pleasant circumstances in your life. We wish you quiet minds. Minds full of the joy of spirit and, until next time, we wish you, with our love, good night.

Red Cloud

I will leave you now. I will leave you with the wish that the Great Spirit embrace you and keep you safe within its wings. I wish you to know the Oneness of the earth, to know the Oneness of the wind, to know the Oneness of the moonlit sky. I wish you all these things and I wish you contentment in your hearts, my friends. Goodnight, my friends.

WB

We will draw things to a close. I wish you peace. I wish you harmony. I wish you an ability to take each step in life as it comes; to live out your days facing each challenge as it comes without a troubled mind; in peace and certainty that you are supported, that you are aided and things work for the best ultimately. I will leave you with these thoughts and wish you peaceful and happy lives. Until we next meet, goodbye.

Isleen

I would give you our blessing and I would hope you would give us yours, for we are all partners in this. We may be a little further up the mountainside sometimes amidst the dancing trees, but the path is the path, which we must all follow; we must all walk and we are partners in this. So I would wish you goodbye and I would wish you particularly joy of life, joy of heart. Goodbye, my friends until we can speak again.

Davia

I wish you all deep peace, gentle peace, the wisdom which comes from peace and from time to time you may find it helpful to hold that great pearl in your hands and meditate on its deep peace and wisdom. I wish you peace. I wish you wisdom. I wish that you may convey this peace and wisdom to the earth, to the people of the earth so that all may feel embraced in its gentleness, in its love, in its wisdom. And until we meet again, I wish you happy hearts and easy minds. Goodbye, my friends.

Hai

And so I wish you, my friends, a blessing of peace. I wish you peaceful minds. I wish you steady minds. I wish you that you keep your hopes, your wishes, and your aspirations in your minds, hopeful expectant, for who knows, who knows what may materialize. And we should be joyful in our lives. We should be hopeful in our lives, for this brings positive energy. This brings positive direction and not negativity. So I wish you well, I wish you peace; peaceful and loving minds. Goodbye, my friends.

*   *   *

And on another night Hai gave us this blessing:

We wish you peace and the love of the One Mind. We wish you the serenity of the One Mind, the embracing of the One Mind. We wish you the peace and tranquillity of the One Mind and the vastness and the stillness of the vast ocean. Goodbye.

About the Authors

After training in the social sciences Paul McGlone embarked on a career in community work. He subsequently moved into Education and Training and had a long career as a Lecturer in the Caring Services. He now has a private hypnotherapy practice. Paul has had a long-standing interest in all religions and sees communication with the spirit world as contributing to the pursuit of Spiritual Truth.

Communications through Paul's trance mediumship are regularly published on his web site. Paul's trance work has prompted a new interest in writing and a number of publications are in preparation, including a novel based on the themes of the spirit communications.

Eileen McGlone worked for over twenty-five years in a Local Authority Social Services Department, as a Social Worker and Team Manager. She became interested in Spiritual Healing in 1981 after she'd received her first healing treatment. Some time later she received training in Spiritual Healing and Reiki. Eileen now works from home. She practices and teaches Reiki, compiles manuscripts of spirit communication and facilitates the meditation and development sessions held at Paul and Eileen's home.

978-0-595-38725-0
0-595-38725-X

Printed in Great Britain
by Amazon.co.uk, Ltd.,
Marston Gate.